DROP THE CHARGES AND YOU CAN GO FREE

Breaking the Chains of Unforgiveness

Many you find the peace of God as you read this book

Joyce Hawk

Joyce Hawkins

DROP THE CHARGES AND YOU CAN GO FREE—
BREAKING THE CHAINS OF UNFORGIVENESS

ISBN (13): 978-1-937632-55-7
ISBN (10): 1-937632-55-5

Library of Congress Control Number: 2013935065

Ebook
ISBN (13): 978-1-93763-258-8
ISBN (10): 1-93763-258-X

Printed in the United States of America

Cover design by Jared Wells

Joyce Hawkins Ministries

Foreword

Throughout the dispensations of life, God always uses a vessel to proclaim an on time, relevant word. The vessel for this dispensation I believe is in the form of Prophetess Joyce Hawkins.

This book that you are about to read is not just for reading, not just for healing, but I believe it is for the WHOLENESS of every broken person.

I highly recommend this book to all who have an ear to hear and a heart to receive!

— Bishop Randall Parker III

DROP THE CHARGES AND YOU CAN GO FREE: Breaking the Chains of Unforgiveness, is a must-read for every man, woman, boy, and girl. This book by Joyce Hawkins is divinely inspired to bring healing to a devastated world and hurting families, but most of all this book forces the body of Christ to face issues that hinder us from maturing in God. As you read this book, allow the Lord to minister to your broken places so He can break and destroy the chains of unforgiveness.

— Pastor Derrick R. Wright

Acknowledgments

I would like to dedicate this book first to the most important person in my life, and that is my Heavenly Father Jesus Christ. He was the one who challenged me to write even when it was difficult to pen the words. Next, I would like to remember some very important people in my life. Although they are gone into the hands of God, they are still in my heart, and without them I would not have been moved to write — my father, Lenon Clark, and my mother, Bettie Ruth Clark. They are the ones who gave me life and love. Then there is my best friend — the man who stretched me through our challenged marriage and caused me to learn to trust God like never before — my deceased husband, Ray Anthony Hawkins. Without meeting him, I might not have known God the way I do, and it was from our union that this book was even possible.

I would also like to thank my son, Derek, and his wife, Amethia, for being patient with me and letting me hide in their spare bedroom as God gave me the words for this book. I want to thank you, Destany, for putting up with me when I had bad days. You are a wonderful jewel that God has given to me. I love you. Thanks to my spiritual sons and daughters Charlene, Melissa, Roger, and Sheena just for being there for me.

I want to also thank my dear friends and extended family: my Godmother, Loretta Wright; and all of my sisters and brothers from that family. Thank you for taking me as your daughter in 1990 when I came to the hills of Tennessee. I want to thank Pastor Derrick and First Lady Sharon Wright of Purpose In Design Ministries for sowing into this project, and for your time, your love, and your financial support. Thanks to my spiritual mother, Mother Arlene Potter, for telling me to stay focused. Thanks to my best friends, Cendy Brooks, Carolyn Smith, Angie Secrest, and Cheryl Threets for their listening ears. I love all of you.

Introduction

There is a book inside of me and I refuse to allow anything or anyone to stop it from coming out. Not even me. I refuse to stand in the way of what God wants to say. So, I am sitting here wondering where to start.

The powerful and anointed Bishop T.D. Jakes wrote a book called *Woman Thou Art Loosed*. This book dealt with the pain of hurting women everywhere. He dealt with women's emotions, their self-esteem, and past and present failures. Bishop Jakes dealt with every area of brokenness that a woman could encounter in life.

Like Bishop Jakes, God has placed in my heart a desire to see hurting men and women gain victory over the scars of past and present failures. He has shown in the Holy Scripture the keys to unlocking the chains of the enemy. Reading this book will help you identify many crippling fears from childhood that may have followed you into your adult life. It will give you answers to questions about broken relationships, which have left many readers in a state of despair and hopelessness, causing you to look for love in the wrong places, people, and things. This book will redirect your love for God and your passion for life.

My desire is for readers of this book to become champions and winners by conquering the things in life that can hold you in emotional and spiritual bondage, thereby keeping you trapped in past failures. I will give the reader the Word of God and my personal experience, which will allow you to break free from the fears that hinder you from moving toward the purpose that God has for your life. These pages will bring you hope so that you can live a life full of peace and joy in Christ Jesus.

Father, in the name of Jesus, thank You for Your loving kindness and Your tender mercies. Oh, how great You are. You have been a real friend and a wonderful Father. Without You, I don't know where I would be and who I would turn to. You have been my hiding place, my shield and fortress; a very strong tower. Life gives so many disappointments and these painful situations caused me to run into Your strong and loving arms. Lord, my soul longs to draw closer and nearer to You each day that I live and breathe. Give me the strength and courage to face the fears of life. Reveal to me the hidden secrets of my heart; the hidden things that have disrupted our intimate relationship. I need You to show me the ungodly things that have caused me not to pursue the wonderful things that You have in store for my life. I thank You for another chance to come before Your throne of grace and mercy. I love You, Father. Continue to work on me, Your loving daughter, Joyce. In the name of Jesus Christ.

Amen

Contents

Chapter One
God, Where Are You and What Are You Thinking?

Jeremiah 29:11— *For I know the thoughts that I think toward you, saith the Lord, thoughts of peace, and not of evil, to give you an expected end.*

The first thing I want to do is thank God for doing all of the important thinking for me that seemed impossible for me to handle. And my important thinking is *everything* that I am thinking. I love God because He is always thinking of me. He is thinking of me even when I fail to think of myself. I confidently believe that His divine plan and views for my life will, in the end, result in me reaching my full potential that He has purposed. His plans will always work for my good. ***Romans 8:28 — And we know that God causes all things to work together for good to those who love God, to those who are called according to His purpose.***

I am grateful that He stepped into my life and took over when He did. It didn't seem like it, but God has been in control of my life at all times. I don't know about you, but many times I struggle with control issues. Let me talk about me, and not you. Many times I have a need to feel that I am in charge. I hate to feel that my life is out of control. Situations and conditions that render me helpless open the doors for great frustration. My life has to have a sense of structure and stability. I just simply hate not knowing where I am going or what I am doing.

So, when I look at my life I see there have been no absolutes. Everything I have ever done was done by faith. That being the case, look at what God does with us. He allows us to feel a sense of control, until we discover that our steps are completely ordered by God — it just didn't look like it at the time. We cannot make one move unless He knows it.

Until we ultimately realize that He is the conductor of our lives, He is standing back watching and waiting for us to get tired of doing it our way. He is there all the time saying, "I have a better plan. Just move out of the way and give your life to Me." That is what I have come to realize; I have never been too far out of His loving reach. I just had to learn to surrender. It was during difficult times that I really didn't realize how much God was thinking about me. But now I understand that I have always been on His mind and He loves me.

Just imagine — God thinking about me! The God of the universe thinking about little old me! One thing I do know for sure is my loving Father continues to think about me. Contrary to some beliefs, the Lord is thinking good thoughts toward us. Even when it doesn't seem like it, God is still thinking good of us. I know some might say, "It doesn't feel like it, because I am going through hell right now!" The pain that you may be facing now might seem like a distorted view of the love of a loving Father like God, but what God sees in us is complete. What we see in ourselves is completely fragmented. We see present *failures* and God sees future *victories*. We see and feel our *now* but God sees and feels our *shall be*. That is why we need to see ourselves through the eyes of God and know His thoughts concerning us.

Isaiah 55:8-9 — *For my thoughts are not your thoughts, neither are your ways my ways, saith the Lord. [9] For as the heavens are higher than the earth, so are my ways higher than your ways, and my thoughts than your thoughts.*

Just think...if God wasn't thinking of us and He left us in charge without His help, picture what the world would be like — and not only the world, but your life.

Let's take a walk on the wild side for a minute just to explore some possibilities. What would we do if God left the world in our hands? Can you imagine if He never intervened? How would you control the oceans, or even the seasons of the year? Wouldn't that be a mess? Jim Carrey starred in a movie call *Bruce Almighty*. His character thought that because of the way his life was going, he could do a better job than God. He continued to complain about the way God was handling things, so God gave him all His powers to use without restraint to teach him how difficult it is to run the world. And he made a mess of things. The mess was so bad that he finally had to admit to God that the job was too big for him to handle.

Let's look even closer at this picture and bring it closer to home. How would you control you? Would you change the total order of things? And by doing so, would the outcome shift life as we know it? What if God allowed every decision we made to be tailored to our desires, whether the decisions were right or wrong? I don't know how you feel, but that is a scary thought to me.

Me...in control! Wow! I have no idea of what I want to do from one day to the next. I have a difficult time just picking out what I would like to wear for the day. And for me to decide what the world would be like in place of God, and to do it for His whole creation — this would just blow my mind! Where would I start and who would I start with? It would be easy to look at someone other than myself, because as humans we can always find fault in others while looking pretty together to ourselves. When I think of that approach, it would leave me in a mess. Everyone else (hopefully) would be doing just fine, and I would still be a hot mess. So you see, that approach is just not going to work for me, which forces me to start with me! Don't get me wrong; it is much easier to start with someone else. Starting with me takes a lot of hard work and pain. It forces me to see the dark side of things that I would hope would never show up. Yes, it requires you to open the Pandora's Box that you have buried in a very secret and dark place for safekeeping. Starting with you causes you to ask some soul-searching questions. Questions like: In what direction is my life headed? Why have I not been able to reach my goals, or see my dreams and desires come true? What or who got me off course? What stopped me and why did I quit? My life is not looking like the thoughts that God is thinking toward me.

4

I thank God that He is still in control. So, He tells you to take a chill pill and shift out of panic mode because He has a plan for your life, and the plan that He has is good. Just think — God is talking to you about the purpose for your life even while your life is spiraling out of control.

Although you would hear His voice under normal conditions, your pain may be screaming louder than His promise to you — and you can't hear past your pain. You are receiving more pain than you are joy and instruction. So, what you think you hear God saying is not what He said. What you are responding to is your pain. While your emotions are driving you to make unhealthy decisions, the quiet voice is saying, "Calm down, I've got this." And if that wasn't enough, to add insult to injury, the Lord tells you to wait.

So, you are thinking, *Wait for what — more pain and disappointment?* This is a question I have asked myself many times: How can I trust the plan when what I see in the plan causes the pain? God, did I hear you right? Trust the plan when the plan is causing the pain? It is at these moments when you cry, "Lord, can you show me what you are thinking? Because what I see, I hope is not what you are thinking."

If this is where you are in life, then you are in the process — and oh, how I hate the process. I would cry, "Lord, can we just skip this part of the plan?" If you are anything like me, you hate the process, because that is where the raw material has to be made into the product or person that God needs it to be. I don't know about you, but I am screaming, "**LORD, GIVE ME THE PROMISE,**

NOT THE PROCESS!"

The process is the place between the call and the promise. God shows you this great and wonderful destiny. He exposes you to a vivid picture of this wonderful and beautiful blessing, so great in its form that you can't wait to receive it. It drives your passion for life to such a degree that you can't seem to get it out of your view. Your whole life becomes consumed with the promise. You hunger and thirst for it so much that it outweighs anything in life. You tell yourself, *When I get my hands on this promise, I will be all right!* Then you wait and wait and wait, and it seems like nothing is happening. You see no evidence of the promise in sight, but God still tells you to wait.

Yesterday I was in the hills of Tennessee with some friends, but when I think of it they are not just friends — they are really my family! We were watching a movie called *127 Hours,* which is based on a real-life event. It was about a climber who had fallen on the ridge of a mountain and his arm was pinned by a large rock. This rock was the only thing standing in the way of his freedom. He tried many times to move it and it was too heavy for him to lift. There were scenes where he would dream of his friends and family to keep his mind off his present condition of suffering. To make a long story short, he got to the point of feeling that death was going to happen at any moment. Then the picture takes a twist and he is shown a glimpse of his future. There set before him was the likeness of a son he had never had. The image that was given to him became his driving force for his desire to continue to exist. It forced him to muster the courage to make a decision that he would not have made under normal conditions. The little boy became the reason for his passion to live. Just one look at his destiny sent him into a passionate pursuit to survive.

You see, God has a great sense of humor. He shows you the end first, and then places a demand on you to walk out the steps to get to what He has revealed. He tells you to start moving in the direction to receive what He has just made known to you. What He didn't let you know was all of the obstacles that would challenge your faith and ability to receive the blessing between the beginning and getting to the promise.

The process is the gray area. It is a place of pain, hard work, and determination. It requires total faith and confidence in God. There are things you must understand about the process to keep you moving in the direction of the promise. And the main thing you need to know is not many things between the initial call or the reveal and the promise make a lot of sense.

It is called a "faith walk." What I want to make perfectly clear is that you must learn to trust totally and completely in God. He is the only light available to you. He is the light of the world. God is the only light that you have to rely on. Without Him there is no light and you find yourself lost and walking in utter darkness.

God tells you that He is going to bless you and make you prosperous, and the only thing you experience is pain and frustration. It may seem that the pitfalls in life have not revealed to you a brighter and better future as God had promised. As a matter of fact, the only thing that you have received so far is the short end of the stick.

It is during these moments that you are left with the lowest point of expectation and you find no hope in sight. You begin to wonder, *Has God abandoned me? I know what He said, I just can't seem to get it to come to pass.* You find yourself at a crossroads in life and you cry, "Lord, what are you thinking? I really need to know what you are thinking."

The life you are experiencing now might be so far from what God said it would be, that it might cause you to question the very voice, will, and intent of God. You stand and say, "Lord, I know what you said, but Lord, I really don't see it coming to pass." Your desire of hope is darkened by constantly struggling with the pain of regret and disappointment and waiting in expectation; especially when you are waiting in a place that looks absolutely nothing like what you were promised. It is then that you reach a low position in life and you are full of uncertainty and insecurities. The love and trust for life have faded and left you with a faint image of hopelessness. These painful life events have left you unable to trust in anyone — even yourself. Then you are clearly introduced to doubt, and any time there is doubt it will always cancel faith — and God said that without faith it is impossible to please Him! Then you ask questions like: Did I hear God right? Was it something that I wanted more than what He really said? Because your dreams and aspirations have been clouded by life's pain and disappointment, the one thing you never stopped to ask God was if that was what He was really thinking concerning you. Remember, He says that the thoughts that He thinks of you are thoughts of peace and not of evil.

Frustrated, you begin to pursue your own future and your own destiny without the leading of the only One that holds the master plan to life. And before you know it, your self-motivated plans for life have navigated you so far away from the purpose and plans that God has for you that you can't see clearly the love, grace, and mercy that your loving Father is extending to you. The choices that you have made have caused you not to take into consideration the desires that God has for your life. Your passion to please yourself became stronger than your desire to surrender to the sweet, loving call of Christ. Jesus said, "I stand at the door and I am knocking." Jesus is knocking because He wants to be a part of your life. He tells us that if we will open the door, He will come in and sup with us. Christ will come in and have sweet fellowship with you.

Once He is in, He will lead and direct you. It is Christ who has the plans for your life. I say again that it is Christ who is thinking about you, and the thoughts He is thinking are thoughts of peace, and not of evil, to bring you to an expected end. When you open up and let Him in, He will tell you what He is thinking about you. He will unfold the plan for your life, and that plan is that you are a winner!

Many are asking, "Is it too late to open the door of my heart?" My answer to you is it is never too late. I want you to understand that as long as you have breath in your body it is never too late. In life, we allow ourselves to get off on the wrong paths and we take the wrong exits. These exits have caused you to run into roadblocks and have changed the very course of your destiny and purpose that God has for you. But always remember that God has a plan. It is God who is thinking good of you even when you are not thinking good of yourself.

Taking these wrong exits and making wrong decisions have caused a domino effect in your life, and you might feel like your life is spiraling out of control. Who is going to stop the pain? That, I feel, is the greatest question. You might feel that there is an emptiness inside, and to be honest, there is. God has a space in your life that only He can fill. Without Him, you are always incomplete.

I want to pause here and make something absolutely clear. You are not the only one who has been in this condition. No, you are not alone. All of humanity has faced this same situation at one time or another because we are all sinful creatures, and we will continue to make ungodly decisions at some point in life. You see, only God can fix the things that are broken in us. The only way that this can be done is for us to surrender our lives totally over to the God who created us.

I would never have imagined that I could be as madly in love with God as I am. But when God Himself walked with me through every painful experience I have ever faced in life, and allowed me to come out a better person, He revealed to me His unconditional love. This allowed me to know that He loved me more than I loved myself.

My life was a great ball of pain. I had babies by different fathers, poverty, bitterness, and very low self-esteem, and the list goes on and on. I was going downhill fast. I was insecure and afraid to trust anyone. I was trying to survive day by day, and worried about dying and going to Hell. Boy, was my life a mess!

Then God stepped in and did for me what was impossible for me to do for myself because I had no long-term plans. I had not even chosen a good retirement plan because the plan that I had chosen, at the end, would cause me to die and go to Hell for eternity. So, I had to trust in God's plan for my life. And thank God I did, because this plan offered great benefits. I had a mansion already prepared. It offered great health benefits, no sickness, no sorrow, no disease, and most of all, no death. But the greatest benefit of all is I get to live with a loving God for all eternity. I learned to accept His love for me and His grace to redeem me. Jesus offered to me the plan of salvation and at that point in life I gladly accepted.

Just think — the God who created the universe is the same God who is willing to deliver you from a destructive existence. He is willing to change the way we live. So, when we have made these horrendous decisions in life, we must run to the throne room of God and fall at the mercy seat. Ask God for forgiveness, and He will lead you to Calvary, where the precious blood of Christ was shed to offer you forgiveness of sin continuously. As long as we admit that we need a savior, and we are sinful and seek forgiveness and mercy, the blood of Jesus cleans, restores, and keeps us until His return. It is His grace and mercy that makes the difference in the life of every child of God.

All of humanity has fallen victim to the trials of life. Scars are very noticeable on some people, and other people have hidden them really well, but believe you me, if you look hard enough we all have scars. Since the fall of man in the Garden, we all battle with our sinful nature. Every person ever born of a woman has been an enemy of God.

Look at the power of forgiveness. Let's think about this for a minute. God wanted to help His enemies. Can you imagine me taking the one object that I loved the most, my prized possession (remember, I really love this thing more than anything in this world), I go to the county jail, and ask, "Do you have my worst enemy in here? Because I want them to be released. I have this one thing that I love with all my heart and I want to offer it for payment for their crime. I am willing to take that priceless gift and pay the price for their crime so that my worst enemy can go free." Doing this (to us) might seem crazy, but to God it is real love. *For God so love the world that he gave his only begotten Son, That whosoever believed in him should not perish but have everlasting life.* That is just what God did for us! He dropped the charges.

Before He sent His son to redeem us from the curse of sin, we were an enemy of His. Not only were we an enemy of His, but we were a slave to sin. We, as humans, are servants to our sinful nature as long as we are without God. Once we accept Jesus Christ as Lord and Savior, and ask Him to come inside of us to rule our lives, we are set free from the bondage of sin. The blood that Jesus Christ shed for us unlocked the prison doors and it set us free.

Sin separates us from God. And as long as we fail to make Him Lord of our lives, we will continue to suffer with feelings of exclusion and disconnection from Him. The effects from the fall of man in the Garden forced humanity to live apart from God. It is sad to say that this one act of disobedience caused humanity to be left with a void in our souls. This severance placed a desire in all of mankind to continually try to seek the relationship that was lost between us and God. So, without Him we look for peace and comfort in everything else but God. As humans we are relentlessly trying to fill the empty place that only God can occupy. We seek for reconnection with God through people, places, and things, hoping to fulfill the lack of God in our lives. These things can never fill the void that only God can satisfy. Our temporary replacements can only magnify the sorrow of our broken relationship with God because they can never measure up to Him, so they continue to leave us empty.

I want to let you know that what you are experiencing did not start with you; it started in the Garden. Unfortunately, we all are born in sin and shaped in iniquity because of disobedience. The problem started with the first family, Adam and Eve. When the serpent had a conversation with Mother Eve about the fruit that God said they could not eat, to her it sounded great when the serpent said that they would be like God and know good and evil. The bible says that she gave to Adam and he did eat. It wasn't Eve who sent us into this horrible state of being, it was our father, Adam. It was when Adam ate that our eyes came open to know good and evil. God gave to Adam the law, but Eve was deceived.

It really doesn't matter how sin came into being. Think of what a costly price they paid for not doing what God said for them to do. Now all of mankind has to suffer for their disobedience. Every child that has ever been born into this world has suffered the effects of their decision. Not obeying God caused them to walk in disobedience and we are now seeing the outcome.

There was also a hidden clause that the serpent did not reveal to Adam and Eve. I hate it when important information is withheld. He failed to tell them that if they were going to be like God and know good and evil, they had to do it without God. Being like God without God is completely impossible.

I want you to take a good look at the heavy price humanity paid in the Garden that day. Once they disobeyed God, they were immediately spiritually disconnected from God. Perhaps they thought it would be a natural death, but the death that they received was a spiritual death. Who can live without His presence? It is impossible to do, because we were created to commune and have fellowship with Him.

Without a relationship with Him we constantly feel the effects of the pain of isolation and lack of communion with our Lord and Savior. Yet, even though we feel this loss of connection and fellowship with God, the good side of feeling this void is it forces us to seek after Him to find completion. We are totally incomplete without Him.

Once we have accepted Him as Lord and Savior, we find comfort and peace in his loving and compassionate arms. Without God, there is a missing part and void in our souls.

It is through our pain we discover that we need God. When we are left helpless to face our sinful selves, with no ability to repair our problems, that is when we search for answers and look to someone who is greater than we are — and that someone is God. He can repair our problems and fill all voids.

It is during these broken, painful, and empty moments that the Lord reveals His loving and caring concern for His creation. The bible lets us know that a broken heart and a contrite spirit He will in no way cast aside. God hears us in our pain and grief. Many times in my life I have asked the question: "God, where are You in all of this pain and sorrow? Have You abandoned me at the lowest time of life? Why are You not answering me? Do You have me on silent?" I have cried, "Lord, please turn the mute button off. I need to hear from You."

It is a very painful experience to go through suffering and not hear or even feel the presence of God. You are frustrated because you cannot tell what God is thinking about your situation, and that can be frightening. At these times when God is not affording you any clear instructions, you will discover that the only thing you can do is wait!

The unexpected loss of a loved one; the pain of receiving divorce papers from a spouse that you thought really loved you; going to the doctor and hearing that you have an unexplained sickness and they don't have a cure; you have the only income in the house, and you go to work and receive a pink slip; your daughter is pregnant and she can't tell you who the father is.... You look for God in every place that you think He can be found. You seek Him in His Word. You go to church to find answers among His people, yet He still seems to be hidden and not talking, so you say once again, "Lord, what are You thinking about me? I know You said they were thoughts of peace and not of evil, but the only thing I feel is hurt and pain. Please let me know the good side of Your thinking."

I want you to know you should not be discouraged, because it is not God who is lost — it is you. You are not looking for Him, it is Him seeking for you. Jesus said that He has come to seek and to save that which was lost. Because of sin, you are the one who has been misplaced and are out of the will of God. He is continuously seeking to place you back into a relationship with Him. His desire is to restore us back as we were before the fall of humanity.

God has had a plan for us from the very beginning of Creation. It has never been His plan that we should be lost. Before the world was formed, He had a lamb to offer as a sacrifice. God knew that man would fail, just as He knew that you and I would fail. Believe it or not, He has had a plan for your life, no matter how bad your life may appear. God loves and still desires to use you if you will allow Him to. You fit into His master plan.

Many are thinking, *I have done so many bad things in my life. How can God desire to use me?* Let me tell you, my dear friend, I have not only done, but have gone through so many bad and horrendous experiences, yet the love and the mercy of God continues to blow my mind. I thought, *Why would God desire to use me after all the mess that I have gone through?* Then I heard other people say that He doesn't hear a sinner's prayer and I felt, *Well, that's the end of that.* I thought, *What's the use? He won't hear me anyway. Why pray?* For a minute I almost believed that lie, until I experienced the love, mercy, and the grace of God for myself. Something within me was telling me, *I love you but I don't love the sin in you.*

Isn't it amazing that with all that we go through in this life, the God of the universe still is madly in love with us? ***Psalm 103:8-14 says: [8] The Lord is compassionate and gracious, Slow to anger and abounding in loving-kindness. [9] He will not always strive with us; nor will He keep His anger forever. [10] He has not dealt with us according to our sins, nor rewarded us according to our iniquities.*** God has not given to us what we deserve to receive for our sins. If God gave to us what we really deserved, then none of humanity would live because the *wages of sin is death,* but the gift of God is eternal life. ***[11] For as high as the heavens are above the earth, so great is His loving-kindness toward those who fear Him. [12] As far as the east is from the west, So far has He removed our transgressions from us. [13] Just as a father has compassion on his children, so the Lord has compassion on those who fear Him. [14] For He Himself knows our frame; He is mindful that we are but dust.*** No matter what happens in my life, God knows me and He loves me. In His sight I am simple dust, but I love Him because He is God. So, as a Father who pities His children, God's love is never-ending. Because of His great mercy He says to us, "Let me clean you up." After He has cleaned you from all of your sins, then you must seek to know Him!

I realized that I was in a bad state of being. And the state that I was in was sin. What a wonderful Savior. He rescued me from eternal damnation. So, I picked up the instruction manual for abundant life. The manual was the bible and I began to read it. The only way that I could really know for myself what God was thinking was to read the manual. And this manual is the Word of God better known to us as the **BIBLE** (**B**=basic **I**=instructions **B**=before **L**=leaving **E**=earth.) God's love and instructions for you are readily available to guide you to a safe and healthy life of prosperity and abundance. Yes, a simple prayer of forgiveness and repentance moves the heart of God. The minute that you decide to change direction and seek for a new way of life, God is there to give you everything that you need. Don't worry about how low you have gone. Begin to be concerned about placing your life in God's hands and see how high He will cause you to soar. The minute you decide to change directions and seek a new life, God is there to give you everything you need.

Some of you might be saying, "How can God use me? I have done so many deviant, wicked, and evil things. It seems impossible for God to love and want to use me." No matter how low you go, God knows His children. We can be covered with the filth of the flesh and the world of sin and shame, but God can see you coming from afar. He knows your walk and everything about you. You are His creation and His child. He will never stop looking and seeking after you. No sin is greater than the other. The bible says *for all have sinned and come short of his glory.* God is so great and powerful and full of mercy that He leaves no room for man to boast in himself. We all are in need of a savior and He loves us so much because His love is everlasting. And this is the wonderful nature of God. He loves us even when we are totally un-lovable. I am glad that He is God and it is in Him that we gain victory.

When we learn to understand what God's plan and the purpose is for our lives, it becomes easy to submit to His will. God's plan and purpose is for us to live with Him for eternity without any suffering, pain, or sorrow. Then and only then will we realize that He is thinking wonderful things concerning us. That is why the prophet Jeremiah tells us in Jeremiah 29:11 that God is thinking thoughts of peace and not of evil to give us an expected end.

When we get to the end of the story, the life of every child of God ends in victory. Please hear me. When Jesus gave His life on Calvary, the cross that He died on brought with it victory. It gave us total redemption. Jesus Christ, the son of God, gave humanity another chance to live throughout eternity. The fall of man brought with it death, but the death of Christ brought with it life eternal!

We think that the height of accomplishment is to be successful in our ministries, talents, and abilities, but the very end of the process and the fulfillment of life and our purpose in God is to live in eternity with Christ. What happened to our desire to keep Heaven in our view? God has always been thinking of man. The whole plan from the beginning was to bring man back into complete fellowship with Him just as we were prior to the fall in the Garden. That is what Calvary was all about.

Calvary was a place of suffering and agony. In the Old Testament the prophet Isaiah foretells the suffering of our loving Savior and he gives to us the purpose of His suffering. In chapter 53 he tells us that Jesus was despised and rejected of men; a man of sorrow and acquainted with grief. He goes on to say that He was wounded for our transgressions, He was bruised for our iniquities, and the chastisement of our peace was upon Him and with His stripes we are healed. What are we healed from? We are healed from sin, suffering, and disease. It does not matter what the problem, condition, or situation is; we are healed because of Christ's sacrifice and His blood. Another thing we are healed from is eternal damnation.

The writer of this chapter continues to expound that yet it pleased the Lord to bruise Him, He hath put Him to grief. When thou shalt make His soul an offering for sin, it pleased God to do this to Christ so that we could live. Before His death, all of humanity was dead. After the death of Christ, by accepting Jesus as the Lord and Savior of our lives, now we can live.

The book of Isaiah tells us that God shall see the travail of his soul and shall be satisfied. Seeing Christ suffering satisfied God for the penalty of our disobedience in the fall of man while in the Garden. Can you see the plan for your life unfolding in the mighty hands of God? He was thinking of you even before you were born. During all of the pain, grief, and sorrow that you have gone through, God has been thinking about you. You have stayed on God's mind and not for one moment have you ever left His thoughts. So, Isaiah goes on to say: **...by his knowledge shall my righteous servant justify many for he shall bare their iniquities.** Once you accept Christ, you are made right with God. Jesus bore our sins and iniquities. No longer will I have to feel the void of seeking for Him and Him seeking after me. Because of His shed blood He is now living within me. The void in my soul is filled by God and He is reigning and ruling on the throne of my heart and soul. That is why the place of Calvary is so important, because Jesus bore our sins and reconciled us back to God. He paid the ultimate price for sin for all of humanity, and that price was paid with His life.

Calvary and the sufferings of Christ occurred because God was thinking about you and me. His plan has always been to bring us to a place of peace with Him. The love that God has for us is so strong that He was willing to sacrifice His only son, and His son was willing to give His only life for us. If God is not thinking about us, then I don't know who is.

So you see, it was in my pain that my loving savior rescued me. During the lowest times of my life, I realized the love of the only real and true God. I discovered that His love is everlasting. God's love is limitless and it never runs out. God is so great that He has enough love to give everyone who will call on His name. The thing that I couldn't do for myself, Jesus did for me. I could not redeem myself, but Jesus did. He paid the price on the cross. The pain of just living life had placed me in an emotional, physical, and mental prison that I could not break free from. The driving factor in my life was my pain and disappointment, and because of these things I sought God like never before. I remembered that His Word said if I seek Him, I shall find Him. So you see, what you could not do for yourself God is more than willing to do for you. He will save you from your sinful nature and give you His Holy Spirit.

Do you see the plan God has had for your life from the beginning? It has always been to offer Jesus as a living and Holy Sacrifice for our sins. I want you to realize God has always been thinking about you and me. We are not an afterthought to God. Before the world was formed, God had Jesus in place to redeem us. Nothing ever slips up on God. So the mistakes and the choices that you have made in life have not caught God off-guard. He was there when you made the mistakes and He is here now to walk you into a greater and brighter future.

The whole totality and thoughts of God are best described in *John 3:16-17 — For God so loved the world, that he gave his only begotten Son, that whosoever believeth in him should not perish, but have everlasting life. [17] For God sent not his Son into the world to condemn the world; but that the world through him might be saved.*

When I think about it, isn't it funny we don't

teach or preach a lot about that anymore? The mention of Calvary or the gospel is almost a byproduct of what we used to hold fast to as the body of Christ. At one point, the church felt that the gospel was the foundation of everything that the ministry of God represented. We clung to Calvary and the blood of Jesus. The old patriots realized that within it came strength and power. Now the aspiration of the body of believers for holding fast to the teachings of the gospel is considered outdated in its theological approach to the body of Christ. But to those who truly understand the power of the gospel and the power of the blood, it is a glimmer of undying hope. Christians who refuse to let go of these teachings are many times considered outdated, self-righteous, and super religious. The church has conformed to the rising economic, emotional, and social needs of our society in our practices and teachings. Many are now looking for methods and techniques on how to build their churches, rather than spend time in the face of God to get the God-given answers on how to heal His people. They don't recognize that teaching and preaching the power of the gospel and presenting to the world the real Kingdom of God, letting the world know that Jesus brought the Kingdom to earth and everything that He was then and still is today, is what the Kingdom of God truly is. Not redefining the gospel, but praying for a greater passion to pursue and chase after the one that brought to us the gift of eternal life. Before Christ died for our sins, all of humanity was truly dead. It is only when we present Jesus to a dying world, and all that He came to earth to fulfill, that there will be effective healing for the nations.

We must begin to teach and preach that Jesus came to earth and presented Himself as a perfect sacrifice without sin. He became the sin sacrifice so that our sins would be forgiven. Jesus placed humanity back in right standing with our Father so that when God sees us, He does not see our sin; He sees His Son's blood. The blood of Jesus washes away our sins and cleans us from all sin. We deserve to die. If we accept Him as Lord and Savior of our lives, He will wash the slate clean and give us an opportunity to become sons and daughters in Christ Jesus.

That is why the battle and struggle that each person that is living, or has ever lived without giving their lives completely over to God, will suffer eternal damnation. This will cause you to leave this world without the promise that God has given to those who follow Him. With the spirit of God within you and leading and directing your course in life, you become a new creation in Christ Jesus. Old things have passed away and all things become new. If you are in the process, remember that it can be painful at times. Just know that His thoughts of you are thoughts of peace and not of evil, to supply you with abundant life and an expected end. Allow your pain to push and stretch you into your purpose and the greatest promise that God will ever have for you. And that promise is eternal life!

Here is a good place to say a prayer:

Father, in the precious name of Jesus, I want to thank You for thinking of me from the very beginning of creation. Even before I was conceived and born You had me on Your mind. The love that You have shown and continue to reveal to me is wonderful and loving. I thank You for allowing Your dear son Jesus to come to earth and die on the cross for my sins. I believe and trust in the blood that Christ shed on Calvary. I now understand that He gave His life for me as a ransom for my sins. I want to accept Him as Lord and Savior of my life. Father, will You please forgive me for all the wrong things that I have done, and I am asking You to blot out all of my sins. Lord, please wash me, and cleanse me from all the wrong things in my life and make me a new creation in You. Come and live on the inside of me. Give me the heart to forgive others as You have forgiven me. God, teach me to love You with my whole heart, mind, body, and soul. Thank You for always thinking of me and teach me to always consider and think of You. I want to live for You and be with You in eternity. These things I ask in the name of Jesus Christ.

Amen

Chapter Two
If This is Really Love, Where Did the Lust Come From?

*N*ow that you understand the sacrifice that God has made to give you hope, take into consideration that there are more steps involved in living for God. You need the full package in order to complete the process and gain victory. What do you do now that you are a Christian and you want to know more about God? Where do you go?

Remember, after you have given your life to Christ and you have become a Christian, you need to find a good bible-based church where you can gather together and learn the Word of God. This will allow you an opportunity to worship and enjoy fellowship with the people of God. The apostle Paul says to the believer in *Hebrews 10:25 — Not forsaking the assembling of ourselves together, as the manner of some is; but exhorting one another: and so much the more, as ye see the day approaching*. It is imperative and very essential to be among God's people and submitted under a Godly covering.

In the day and age that we live in, we have the Internet, Twitter, Facebook, and television evangelists, pastors, and teachers. These resources are wonderful tools in ministry, but they were never designed to replace the local assembly and the connection that we should have to the body of

Christ. There is something about being in the company of fellow believers in Christ and seeing our Father's glory revealed among us that is indescribable. No experience can compare or take its place.

We come together and build healthy relationships; relationships that will hold us accountable to the Word of God that has been spoken over our lives and through the Holy Scriptures. These deposits of truth make us responsible to live a Godly life. We learn to pray for each other and encourage one another. We also become examples to others. I don't know what I would do without my sisters and brothers in the Lord. Many of them have richly blessed my life.

I want you to understand that although there are great benefits in our coming together as the body of Christ, there are also major pitfalls and disappointments. That is why I am writing this, so you can be aware. I wouldn't dare let you think that you are walking into a perfect world or among perfect people. We are somewhat of a dysfunctional family, yet we are redeemed by His blood. Our accepting Him as Lord and Savior gives us the liberty to go boldly before His throne and ask of His mercy, grace, and His cleansing power. That is why I dare not paint for you a picture of total perfection now that you have surrendered your life to Christ. As I said in the previous chapter, this is a process and we are all in it until we die. I want you to see a clear view of who you are and the journey that you have begun to embark on in the body of Christ.

What I will write in these few pages will be a very sensitive subject. I want to be careful not to discourage the new convert or anyone reading this book. I don't want you to walk away feeling as if the power of God to change us is not real; or what is the use of living for God when there are so many indiscretions? There is no hurt like church hurt (which is when you have fellowship with believers and they present themselves without compassion and no Godliness; they disappoint and discourage).

You might think, *I didn't come here for this, I just came to serve and live for God.* But in the process, you are going to have some disappointing moments. It is no different than attempting to build a relationship with someone you just met. There are going to be good days and bad days. The bible says that if we are to reign with Him, then we have to suffer with Him.

Much of the pain you feel while you are in the world you might have expected to feel because of the nature of the people you were among. But when you gave Him your life, He promised you a more fruitful life. You understand that ungodly people behave in an ungodly manner because they are without Christ. But when you get to the house of God, you never expect to be wounded by the people who say that they have the mind, heart, and desires of Christ.

What happens when you see things in the house of God that are not Godly? How do you handle them? After all, these are the people who are giving us the pain, and they just happen to be our sisters and brothers in the Lord. We have the same spiritual bloodline, yet we find people who plot and scheme and hurt one another as though we are not in the family, or even a part of the body.

Even Jesus said in ***Matthew 12:48-50*** *— "Who is my mother and who are my brothers?" [49] And stretching out His hand toward His disciples, He said, "Behold, My mother and my brothers!" [50] "For whoever does the will of My Father who is in Heaven, he is my brother and sister and mother."* Even though Jesus makes this statement, He has chosen men who have character flaws and at times did not behave Godly; yet, He did not dismiss them from their assignment. You are not just called, but you are *chosen* of God. Just as you are a work in process, so are your sisters and brothers, and God is aware of it all. Always remember that no matter what happens, there is still hope. It is God who is the righteous judge, and we all carry some baggage to the table.

I would like to bring to your attention a story in the bible about a sister and a brother. In this story, the brother brought much pain to his sister and family. The name of the girl was Tamar. The story of Tamar is one of the most heartbreaking stories I have read. Tamar did not fall victim to her enemies, but she fell victim to her own family. Many times we don't fall victim to the people outside of the church; it is the people in the church that hurt us the most. Remember, the church has become our new extended family. So, let's look at her story.

II Samuel 13:1-20

And it came to pass after this, that Absalom the son of David had a fair sister, whose name was Tamar; and Amnon the son of David loved her. [2] And Amnon was so vexed, that he fell sick for his sister Tamar; for she was a virgin; and Amnon thought it hard for him to do anything to her. [3] But Amnon had a friend, whose name was Jonadab, the son of Shimeah David's brother: and Jonadab was a very subtle man. [4] And he said unto him, Why art thou, being the king's son, lean from day to day? Wilt thou not tell me? And Amnon said unto him, I love Tamar, my brother Absalom's sister. [5] And Jonadab said unto him, Lay thee down on thy bed, and make thyself sick: and when thy father cometh to see thee, say unto him, I pray thee, let my sister Tamar come, and give me meat, and dress the meat in my sight, that I may see it, and eat it at her hand. [6] So Amnon lay down, and made himself sick: and when the king was come to see him, Amnon said unto the king, I pray thee, let Tamar my sister come, and make me a couple of cakes in my sight, that I may eat at her hand. [7] Then David sent home to Tamar, saying, Go now to thy brother Amnon's house, and dress him meat. [8] So Tamar went to her brother Amnon's house; and he was laid down. And she took flour, and kneaded it, and made cakes in his sight, and did bake the cakes. [9] And she took a pan, and poured them out before him; but he refused to eat. And Amnon said, Have out all men from me. And they went out every man from him. [10] And Amnon said unto Tamar, Bring the meat into the chamber, that I may eat of thine hand. And Tamar took the cakes which she had made, and brought them into the chamber to

Amnon her brother. *[11]* And when she had brought them unto him to eat, he took hold of her, and said unto her, come lie with me, my sister. *[12]* And she answered him, Nay, my brother; do not force me; for no such thing ought to be done in Israel: do not thou this folly. *[13]* And I, whither shall I cause my shame to go? And as for thee, thou shalt be as one of the fools in Israel. Now therefore, I pray thee, speak unto the king; for he will not withhold me from thee. *[14]* Howbeit he would not hearken unto her voice: but, being stronger than she, forced her, and lay with her.

[15] Then Amnon hated her exceedingly; so that the hatred wherewith he hated her was greater than the love wherewith he had loved her. And Amnon said unto her, Arise, be gone. *[16]* And she said unto him, there is no cause: this evil in sending me away is greater than the other that thou didst unto me. But he would not hearken unto her. *[17]* Then he called his servant that ministered unto him, and said, Put now this woman out from me, and bolt the door after her. *[18]* And she had a garment of divers colours upon her: for with such robes were the king's daughters that were virgins apparelled. Then his servant brought her out, and bolted the door after her.

[19] And Tamar put ashes on her head, and rent her garment of divers colours that was on her, and laid her hand on her head, and went on crying. *[20]* And Absalom her brother said unto her, hath Amnon thy brother been with thee? But hold now thy peace, my

***sister: he is thy brother; regard not this thing.
So Tamar remained desolate in her brother
Absalom's house.***

This story begins by identifying Tamar as
the beautiful sister of Absalom. Her appearance
was so radiant that it sparked an unnatural love in
her brother Amnon; so much so that he became sick
for her. The scripture says that his desire for her
was love, but I call it lust. Tamar was a virgin and
was innocent. She had never experienced the
sensual touch of a man. And it grieved Amnon that
he could not have her.

The bible tells us that Amnon loved Tamar,
but in reality it was plain old lust. Let me identify
that old ancient spirit of lust. It has been around
for a long time. To lust is to have a very strong
desire to obtain or have something or someone. It is
about possession and greed. The relationship of
Tamar and Amnon as sister and brother was not a
relationship that showed the love that a brother
should have for his sister; rather, it was a cruel
display of lust.

Guess what? We have those same relationships in the church today. It is not always a
relationship where a man or woman is lusting in a
sexual manner. Sometimes they lust after titles,
positions, anointing, and attention. Yes, in the
house of God there are people who lose sight of the
mission and purpose of God. So, don't be shocked if
you see these things happening.

You say you love me, but you lust after my
husband or my wife. You say you love me, but you
can't celebrate my accomplishments. You hate to
see my gifts, talents, and abilities, but you say that

you love me. And more often than not you wish it was you! If this is really love, then where did the lust come from?

That is why the picture must be clearly painted. I must let you know that in the house of God, sometimes we see relationships that are not healthy or even in perspective with the will of God. While walking with God I have come to know that the church is not a perfect environment. But when you think about it, neither is our home, our job, our community, or our world. No place is perfect! So don't come looking for perfection — come seeking God.

As believers, when we enter into our relationship with God we must learn to see things in a realistic view, understanding that we are still human and we do err. Okay, I said it. We are not yet perfect. We love God, but we don't always do Godly things. The secret is out! Now what? Contrary to popular belief, there are no super saints. God uses broken vessels. He is the one who makes us new. That is what makes our relationship with Him so wonderful. He does for us what we cannot do for ourselves.

So, in knowing this truth we should pursue Him knowing that we are a work in progress and are not yet perfected. If we really understand the real need of God, then our real expectations will allow us room to understand that there is a capacity of error in the Christian environment. Not only is there error in the Christian environment, there is error within each and every one of us. That is why we cannot afford to panic and quit when we see things that we think are not in alignment with what God said.

Being in the house of God with broken people such as yourself, and understanding that they are fighting to overcome things in their lives the same way that you are, should give you more determination to trust not in man, but in God.

Don't be afraid when you, as a believer, experience the attack of the enemy from someone determined to please themselves with a lustful and selfish passion. Don't be alarmed and quit. Just know that God is still in control. Remember that the reason you are hearing and seeing these things happen within the body of Christ is because you, as a believer, have decided to be committed to serve God and live for Him, and He has shown you these things to pray about so that you can strengthen not only yourself, but your brothers and sisters, as well. The moment you decided to live a Godly life, you should know that your enemy immediately committed himself to destroy your desire to please God. And he will use anything and anybody to try to pull you away from God.

The antics that Satan uses are deplorable. He will take any opportunity to wreck your relationship with God. That is why lust is very shrewd and cunning. That is why I want to distinguish the severe consequences of this spirit and the effects that it has on others. In the situation between Amnon and Tamar we find that his lust was an unrestrained sexual craving.

Lust is a very cruel enemy. The desire — or should I continue to say "the lust" — that Amnon had for Tamar was completely focusing on him pleasing himself with no regard for the consequences. There was no way he could have loved Tamar, because when we continue to read the story his actions only displayed the works of lust. What a shame and a pity that Amnon could not respect the family boundaries and treat his sister with the love and compassion that God would have required from him. His selfish display changed not only Tamar, but it affected their whole family.

That is the way the mishandling of our sisters and brothers in Christ is. Not only do we damage one another, but when it is over, the whole body of Christ is bleeding and wounded. It is impossible for me to be in the presence of someone who is hurting and not feel anything from their pain. When we bite and devour one another for selfish motives and lustful gain, we weaken the unity of fellowship among the believers. It causes disunity. Always remember, God never leaves us without hope.

There is a flipside to every evil thing, and that is good. God has a counter weapon for every attack, and that weapon is the spirit of love. Love has the ability to cancel any evil deed and cause you to recover your hopes and dreams. It is like medicine for the soul. Real love releases you from the pain, although many times we want to call lust love, but their characteristics are not the same.

It frightens me that the word "love" has been tossed around so loosely that the real meaning has lost its significance. The power of love is so great that the whole gospel is based on it. *For God so loved the world that he gave his only begotten son that whosoever believed in him shall not parish but have everlasting life.* Paul so clearly describes it in the 13th chapter of I Corinthians. This chapter paints a picture of the full essence of love. It describes its power and the long-suffering that it contains. If you have ever really been in love, then you understand that love suffers long and is kind. Then it goes on to say that love envieth not, vaunteth not itself, and is not puffed up. Love does not behave itself unseemly. Real love has a way of presenting itself so that it will not hurt or wound others.

Let's be real. I love snacks like cookies, chocolates, and I have a love for unhealthy food. It wasn't my *love* for these things that was hurting me; it was my *lust* for them that was killing me. My lust caused me to reach 300 lbs. Even though there was more going on internally than my love for junk food (we will talk about that in a later chapter) my pain caused my love to become my lust. It became my place of comfort. Amnon's pain for the unnatural love for his sister Tamar turned into a lust for her. He was pain-driven. The bible says that he was vexed and became sick. That sickness turned into lust. When lust goes unchecked and you never get to the root of the matter, it can become deadly. Lust kills, especially if it is the wrong type of lust. The bible tells us in ***James 1:14-15 ...but every man is tempted, when he is drawn away of his own lust, and enticed. [15] Then when lust hath conceived, it bringeth forth sin: and sin, when it is finished, bringeth forth death.*** Lust is very deadly. It kills any dreams and desires that you may have for your future because lust can grip your every thought. It can capture your every waking moment, and it will fight you even in your sleep. That is why the bible tells us to guard against the lust of the flesh, the lust of the eye, and the pride of life. These are the things that destroyed us in the Garden, and they are still alive and well today. They are killing many of our loved ones. Our churches are dying, and so are our communities and the fabric of our nation.

If you will just go with me and see clearly, you might ask, "What was kind about him plotting to rape his sister?" Or, "What was decent about him even having that type of immoral desire for his sister? Sounds like lust to me." By this description, it really is not sounding like Amnon was in love. And by raping Tamar, he sure fit the category of "unseemly." Isn't it funny that a person can desire something so much that they lose all sense of reality and their sense of moral conduct? Amnon's behavior reminds me of that of an addictive personality.

I say this because I have had firsthand experience of living with a man with an addiction. Crack cocaine was my husband's drug of choice. He would do some of the dumbest things that you could ever imagine while under the influence of the drug. I remember once when we were having a wild game dinner for the church. He volunteered to supply the dinner with quail and many of the wild meat dishes because he loved to hunt and fish. He and my pastor were good friends and he convinced the pastor to buy him some live quail to use to train his hunting dog, Betty. These birds would serve two purposes; one was for training and the other for cooking. After training Betty and teaching her with the birds, he would then kill the birds and clean them for the dinner.

A few days before the dinner his drug
addiction clicked in and he was off and running.
When I got home from work that day, the garage
(which had been full of birds) was suddenly empty.
My husband returned a few days later. He finally
got home off of one of his "runs." (This is the term I
would often use in referring to these missing-in-
action times.) I asked Ray, "Where are the birds for
the wild game dinner?"… seeing that there was no
sign of them in the house. His reply was, "I took
them to the vet because they were really sick." Me
being a city girl and unfamiliar with wild game,
because the only thing my parents ever cooked that
was wild was rabbit and raccoon, I didn't know
anything about quail. I thought for a minute maybe
they were sick. Okay. To be honest, I think my
husband took advantage of my lack of knowledge of
country living. He knew I really didn't know.

As days passed by, and not seeing any quail,
I asked him one day after he had picked me up
from work, "Don't you think we need to go and
check on the birds?" Although something within me
was screaming that we were going on a wild quail
chase, being new to all of the madness I wanted to
believe in him. After all, we are talking about
something that was meant to be an enjoyment for
the church. Surely he feared God more than to steal
from Him like that.

Even though deep down inside I felt that
there were no birds to check on, I had to finish the
process to see if I could get the truth from him. You
know women — we have to keep asking until we
hear the truth. It is like the affair that you know

your husband is having. Even though you see all the signs that are pointing to the affair, you want to hear it *from him*. Well, that was where I was. I wanted him to tell me the truth, even though I saw all the signs.

His reply was, "We'll go by the vet's now to see if the birds are all right." And he took me to a house with several puppies in a pen and told me that this was the vet's house. It was the country, and I didn't know anything about country living. After all, the only country I had experienced was on television. So, I thought maybe they had vets that worked out of their beautiful homes.

My husband told me to wait in the car, because he was going to check on the birds. He came out with a man, but no birds. Then they went to the pen, which was full of English Setter puppies, and picked out a beautiful male puppy. I would later discover that the house we were at was not the vet's, although he was a doctor, and there were no birds in the house for my husband to check on.

What we did leave there with was another hunting dog that my husband called Hank. Thinking back now, I should have known better. Well, he stuck to his story that the birds were too sick to eat and they had to be put to sleep. So, the pastor bought more birds — this time frozen and ready to cook.

We laughed about it some years later before he died. I asked him if he remembered the birds, and telling me that he took them to the vet, and he said no. We had a big laugh, but at the time he did it, it was painful. It sounded so foolish that even he could not believe he had done that.

Even though, while we were in the middle of the madness, I knew that he was lying when I confronted him, I wanted to see how far he would go to cover up his lies. Do you see the madness of lust? It breeds with it lies and deception.

In one sense, he was a very loving guy, but when the lust for drugs would overtake him you cannot believe the things he would do. At those moments nothing seemed important to him, not his family or himself. It was all about satisfying his thirst for crack cocaine. Whatever it took for him to get it was all that could be realized at these moments. His lust, strong passion, and desire were all that he could think of at that time. His addiction became his reality and everything that he could use to satisfy the addiction was what he focused on — the same as with Amnon and Tamar; having Tamar was all Amnon could see. At that moment, his perverted thoughts for Tamar became his reality. The passion to please the flesh became more important to him than to do the will of God.

Some of you might say that this is the way of the world. These are their standards. The world operates like that. The people who know God and have been in the church know better. Is it possible to be in the church and still struggle with lust? Tamar and Amnon were family members, but Amnon was overtaken by his lust.

Let me get real with you. My husband was a pew baby, and if anyone knew church, he did. His whole family had a history of church involvement. It was me who didn't know much about church when we married. The only thing I knew was I was glad to be out of the Devil's hands and in the hands of a loving God.

Just being honest; I am glad that I no longer do church. I attend church, but I do not go to church looking for all of the man-made legalistic laws that God is not requiring that we obey. But I have learned to hear His voice and follow Him. I understand what it is to have a relationship with God. I am not talking about assembling together with other believers and calling it church; what I am saying is that I refuse to put limits on God's grace and mercy. I refuse to allow anyone to make me believe that God is sitting around waiting for me to fall and make a mistake, and to count me out, when He sacrificed so much to include me. God paid an awful price for me and I won't allow self-righteous people to make me believe that my weaknesses, which I am praying about every day, will stop God from loving me. The Devil is a liar.

My husband would constantly say "that is not holiness" because he was so driven by strict rules — so much so that he couldn't understand intimacy or relationships. What I took as an opportunity for God to pen my life and turn it into a wonderful story, my husband saw as being stuck and he could not get past his pain and frustration, or the church and their rules. While I presented to God a blank page, my husband presented to God a full page. He kept reliving his past failures. I offered God the blank pages of my life so that He could write and shape my relationship with Him.

What I understood was that the blood of Jesus had washed away my past, leaving only empty pages before God and I was now in a position that God could write my life any way He chose to. I surrendered these pages of my life to Him so that He could fill them with His wonderful plans for my future.

My husband was still carrying his past and all of the games that it had taught him, never finding quiet times with God to receive His instructions for his future. He could never experience a sense of freedom because he honored the laws that man had placed on him, and not the will of God for his life. He could not accept the grace of God, because when he failed he would not receive God's forgiving grace. He believed that he had to perform duties to be set free from his failures and sins. What my sweet husband did not understand was that grace is all you need. So, he held on to the pain of falling into his fleshly desires that separated him from God. He could not grab hold of the one key ingredient of the gospel, and that is simple forgiveness. One of the last things that Jesus did while hanging on the cross was to look at humanity and say, "Father, forgive them for they know not what they do." At that point, Jesus released humanity and humanity released Him to fulfill His destiny to redeem the world with no guilt of harboring unforgiveness. That was something that Satan could not tempt or hold Him in prison with. When Jesus forgave us, He was dropping the charges.

When you drop the charges, you can go free — free to go and do all the things that God has planned for you to do, be, and become. My husband never learned to forgive himself, and since he could not manage to forgive himself, he struggled with applying forgiveness to others. He just couldn't comprehend the meaning of forgiveness or the grace that God gives us — a simple principle that seems so hard to grasp.

The grace of God is God's unmerited favor. He gives kindness when we don't desire it. What we should deserve, God does not apply to our lives, but grace forgives. For our sins we deserved to die, but God did not give us the death penalty. He allowed us to live. My husband saw his life falling apart and he could not trust in the grace of God to hold it together. So, on the pages of his life he saw grace dimly. The things that were in clear view for him were his past and his failures. Don't get me wrong; he was faithful to the church, attending church Sunday after Sunday. It appeared that the only things he could grasp were the laws and duties that the church offered. He could never see his freedom in God. And if you don't see your freedom in God, you leave God no blank page to write on.

Many of the things that remained on his pages were his failures and mistakes; the church's rules, their doctrines, and please don't let me forget their dress codes (which I often broke, and he couldn't understand why). While he was in bondage by the church laws, I was walking in freedom by God's grace.

My husband left no space for God to write or speak to him about the power of forgiveness, and when he did, it was clouded by what he was taught and believed. When we settle for religion and self-righteous beliefs, blinded to the fact that they are against the very nature and the compassion of God, undoubtedly we fail to leave space to repent and forgive. By doing this, it leaves God no room to rule in our lives.

It is only when we walk in forgiveness with a true relationship and fellowship with God that He gives us the faith to believe that He has the power and has given us His grace to overcome our areas of weakness. Without accepting the knowledge of His mercy and accepting His abundant grace, it leaves our flesh screaming louder — much louder than the power within us to believe that the grace of God can and will keep us. We become flesh-driven and not God-driven, and in doing so we are driven by the lust of the flesh.

The lust of the flesh will only feed its appetite with things that it loves, not seeking any instruction from the mind of God, totally relying on its own will, feeling a sense of entitlement to what it wants, needs, and expects. Lust is very self-serving and self-centered. It is all about pleasing the self. Lust will never, ever think about anyone else. Before I go any further, I want to make sure that you understand that I am speaking about fleshly lust and not a strong lust for God.

That is why addictive people have such a strong fixation for their addiction, whether it is drugs, alcohol, pornography, work — whatever it may be. I believe that a door of pain has been opened, and no one seems to be able to help get it closed. So, they relive the struggle of their souls. The recorder never stops rewinding and their addiction becomes the numbing for their pain. They are constantly trying to cover the pain, so they get lost in the process of not accepting forgiveness for their actions. They refuse to forgive others for their offenses because they have a hard time forgiving themselves. Many addictive people find it difficult to believe that God will forgive them so freely. By holding on to unforgiveness, they refuse to release the pain and hurt that someone else has caused to them. Their escape from reality is fueled by their internal pain. So, their addiction becomes their reality. The desire or passion for the addiction consumes every rational decision that they may encounter. They are willing to do anything to fulfill their lustful obsession. Many lose themselves in their lust and unhealthy passions. By yielding to their obsessions, many are willing to hurt themselves, and also destroy others. They are so blindly guided by their lustful appetites and crazy desires that they refuse sound counsel from others. Oftentimes they are living in a fantasy world, and the only thing they can see is what they are lusting after.

My husband would always talk about the things that happened in his past — the pain of rejection and his failures. The little boy that was within him kept him lost and looking at his past, so much so that he was unable to find the man who was standing in front of him. He could never see what God wanted him to become. His reaction to the pressures of life forced him to reach for a comforting pacifier, and that pacifier was crack cocaine. If only he could have stopped for a moment, and allowed the healing of God's grace (which none of us deserves, but which any of us can receive), his healing would have been complete and the chains of his addiction would have been broken. If we don't learn to accept the healing and forgiveness of God, we wind up hurting those around us. Our gaping sores have a way of infecting those around us — especially the ones we love. So, we must learn to turn to God and ask for His help and His healing.

Let's stop and pray:

Father, in the name of Jesus we come asking You for help as only You can. The pain of unforgiveness is so heavy and the burden that comes with it is much more than we can bear. Many are looking for comfort in things other than You, Lord. Give us the desire to accept Your grace, love, comfort, and forgiveness. Release us from our past rejections. Give us the ability to forgive others as You have forgiven us. We know that it is by Your grace that we are still here today and we thank You for that.

Pull the layers of sorrow and pain off of us. Remember those that are ensnared by the trap of the enemy of addiction. Whether it is crack cocaine, alcoholism, pornography, being a workaholic, food addictions, and so many more, break them free. Break the chains and yokes of bondage off of them right now. Help them to learn to accept Your gift of salvation. Make them to become sons and daughters. Place them in a relationship with You as their loving

Father. Become Lord of their lives and live within them as You are living and breathing in me. Give them a heart that burns for You and take full control of their lives until they see no more of themselves, but they begin to see only You.

We love You, Father, and we appreciate Your goodness. These things we ask in the name of Jesus Christ.

Amen

Chapter Three
I Didn't Come Here for This

*I*f there ever was a time to be real, the time is now. We, as the people of God, are great pretenders. We do a very good job at masking our pain and the real issues and challenges that we face in everyday life. Not only do we wear masks in life, but we have become great pretenders in the church.

Many of God's people run from the call of God. They neglect the purpose that God has placed upon their lives. Oftentimes we settle for the comfortable and mundane rather than the uncomfortable. The reason we settle for the comfortable and mundane is because the uncomfortable leads us to pain. And as crazy as it may seem, our pain forces us to totally seek, depend, and rely on God.

I learned that with God, if a thing is easy, it is probably not God. God always stretches us past our capabilities and capacity. He pulls us until it hurts. God stretches us until our *normal* appears *abnormal* to the world.

That is why in this season God is placing a demand on the body of Christ. The demand is to become the church that He has called us to be. He is pulling and stretching us to reach our full potential and radically reach the world for Christ.

We have been given a mandate to share the gospel of Jesus Christ to all of God's creation. We also have to demonstrate God's power and His ability to deliver those who are in bondage. The world has to see the power of God demonstrated through us. We have to reveal to a hurting society that God is still in control and that He is the true redeemer.

When you are playing in a game and you get to the last few minutes, the coach says to the team, "This is crunch time." We have to play good offense and good defense if we want to win. Men and women of God have to seek God for strategies that will reveal His heart and share His truths. Jesus says, "I came that you might have life and might have it abundantly."

Let's go back to the simple gospel and Calvary. It has always worked; and besides, it's been proven. This will heal our churches and win people over to Jesus Christ (those who don't know Him). What I am saying to the body of Christ is, this is crunch time in the Kingdom of God, and we will not be going into overtime. If a soul dies without receiving Christ as Lord of their lives, there is no other opportunity. It is over and done. What a sad thought, to live in this life and die without God.

I had a brother at our church say to me, while looking at one of my messages that I spoke, "Evangelist Joyce, I bet you can really preach on the blood." I was amazed because the way he said it was as if a message on the blood was outdated and old-fashioned. I am not an outdated or an old-fashioned preacher. I just understand the power of the blood because it was the blood that saved me!

The church sings a song that says: What can wash away my sins? Nothing but the blood of Jesus! What can make me whole again? Nothing but the blood of Jesus! Oh, precious is the flow that makes me white as snow. No other fount I know. Nothing but the blood of Jesus! It is the blood that saves, heals, and delivers. That is what will heal and deliver this world in these last days! We must go back to the cross and the blood — please!

If there ever was a time that we needed the blood, that time is now. The saints of old would stand in times of trouble and say to the Devil, "I plead the blood." If the Devil showed up in a service, the old blood-washed patriots of God would not be moved, but would drive the demons out. They would stand flat-footed and plead the blood, because they knew that there was power in the blood. It is time for the real church to plead the blood!

In a court of law you have to make a plea. You can either plead guilty or not guilty, although many times before you make your plea the prosecuting attorney offers you a deal. It is called plea bargaining. They allow you to accept a lesser charge.

That is what Calvary is. It is a plea bargain. We were facing the death penalty, but God offered us a plea bargain. In the natural court of law, if you accept the plea bargain, the sentence is reduced. But with God, if you accept the plea, and declare, "Lord, I am a sinner and I have sinned. I need a savior. I accept your son Jesus Christ as Lord and savior," your sentence will not be reduced, but He will drop the charges and your debt will be paid in full. Men and women, we are guilty, and it is time for us to make a plea. We need to plead the blood and accept the deal.

It was the blood of Jesus that caused God to drop the charges! Jesus took His precious blood to the mercy seat of God and made an atonement for our sins. And then and only then did God drop the charges. We were guilty. We deserved to die, but the blood paid the price so we could live!

That is why the enemy wants us to move away from Calvary and the blood! But the real prophets are here and sent by God to sound the alarm in Zion. Go back to the blood and use its power! We are not prophesying houses and cars and husbands and wives, but what we are crying is repent and be saved! The end-time prophets are crying, "The time is at hand for the coming of the Lord. He is coming back!"

The true prophets are not sedating you with messages of encouragement, but they are crying holiness or Hell. It is past the time of feeling good. It is time to live the life that God requires us to live and stand for righteousness and have some integrity. These men and women of God are crying, "Walk away from the old man, and allow God to make you new."

We don't need cars and houses. The world can give us that. But what we do need is eternal security and that only comes through the blood. We will get houses and cars and our desires if we walk upright before Him. He will give us the desire of our hearts. The bible tells us that it is His good pleasure to give to us the Kingdom.

As children of God, if we learn to follow the plan of God these things will come. Trust me on this one. But what we do need is the power of God moving in the earth realm! To drive out darkness and the deception of the enemy! We need the blood of Jesus!

This is the formula that was given to us by Jesus Christ Himself, and it has been proven. It defeated death, Hell, and the grave, and put Satan to open shame. Jesus took the keys and declared that all power in Heaven and earth belonged to Him. The blood will work if we work it. And besides, if we are going to gather the harvest, we have to use the power of the blood. The songwriter Andrea Crouch says that it will never lose its power. His lyrics go like this: **The blood that Jesus shed for me, way back on Calvary, the blood that gives me strength from day to day, it will never lose its power. It reaches to the highest mountain, it flows to the lowest valley; the blood that gives me strength from day to day, it will never lose its power.**

There is a mandate by God that we must gather the end-time harvest, and it is not an option. This is the season when we have to go and take back our families. We have to be determined to come against every generational curse coming against us, leaving a legacy that stands and declares that the curse stops at my house and it will not be passed on to my children. As Joshua declared, "As for me and my house, we will serve the Lord!"

That is why we have to start in our homes, our neighborhoods, our schools, communities, and churches. We have to take back our families, and especially our churches. Somewhere we got lost and off track from the will of God. We lost focus of the real plan, and that real plan is to reconcile humanity back to God.

Whether we want to believe it or not, there are still people who desire to be saved. The bible lets us know that the harvest is plenteous but the laborers are few. No matter what we see in the world there is a harvest. We just have to seek God to show us how to reach them.

But is the church prepared for this assignment? Are we ready to receive the fruit that God will send? The reason I ask these questions is because we have already wounded and bruised the fruit before it enters the house of God. The world is not just hurting because of what is going on in it; the world is wounded by the house of God.

The world is not dying because people are killing each other; the world is dying because we are failing to give people the hope that they need. It is not the natural death that disturbs me; it is the eternal separation from God that frightens me.

The enemy knows that as long as he keeps us fighting each other, he can destroy our loved ones. And if you are anything like myself, you did not give your life to God to fight in the house of God. You are probably saying, **"I didn't come here for this!"**

That is why the enemy has kept us distracted with each other in the house of God to such a degree that we have lost sight of the real call of God. Satan understands that if we give this world Jesus, then the senseless killings will end. Families will be healed and broken relationships mended. Marriages will be restored. Our children will change their generation, and generations to come.

So, you see, the world is not being hurt by individuals only; they are being hurt by the **church!** The church should be a place where people should be healed. But we have allowed it to become a place where we are being wounded. I have heard people say that the church is the only place that kills its wounded, but if we repent and turn back to God, it doesn't have to be like that.

Hear me clearly — as believers we have done an injustice to our society because of the misrepresentation of the gospel. Because what we call "the gospel" is not the gospel. It is a bundle of flesh and emotions. These messages are soothing and comforting and they leave us with a temporary high. They never penetrate the heart; they stir the flesh. So, by the time we get home and deal with the real issues, we have no strength to withstand the attacks of the evil one. I am tired of shallow messages that speak to our emotions and do not penetrate our hearts, our spirits, or our souls. Many are preaching messages telling us to turn around and you will turn out of it. Take a step and you just move out of your situation. These messages only leave us with physical and emotional demonstrations, and not a spiritual encounter with God. If that is all the message has to offer, then that message will only excite our emotions and leave our spirit uncultivated and very mal-nourished.

What happened to us getting to the core of the matter (sin)? It was sin that separated us from God. And it is sin that is keeping us from pleasing Him and receiving the blessings that He has for us. The thing that we refuse to deal with is the very thing that is destroying us. If we deal with the sin, then our emotions will be healed because it is the sin that blocks the power of God from operating in our circumstances. Sin is the assassin; it is the hit man; it kills all things.

So, the message we receive to heal our emotions can never reach that place of pain because sin has blocked it from penetrating our heart, and sin stands in the way of our healing.

That is why, when I wanted to be helped and I followed the instructions of the man or woman of God, I couldn't receive the healing because I didn't have an *emotional* problem, I had a *sin* problem and a *flesh* problem.

If they said "turn around," I did. I turned around and I moved out of the place I was standing in at the house of God until I was dizzy, hoping that things would change, being obedient to the preacher, and believing every word they said. I followed their every instruction, but nothing moved or changed at home. When I got home, I still had a husband with a crack cocaine habit. I wasn't fighting my emotions; I was fighting a man full of sin and the desires of his flesh.

I am sure some of you are asking, "What happened?" I am glad you asked. I got real with God, suited up for battle, and began to fight. It was not until I found my prayer closet in my living room and read the Word of God that changes began to happen. Then and only then was I able to bear up under the pressure of the attacks of the enemy.

If God was going to solve my emotional problem, He had to first resolve the sin problem. I had to be able to identify my enemy and understand who and what I was in battle with. By knowing my enemy, then and only then could I hear the Word of God that would heal my emotions.

Sin brings condemnation, oppression, un-forgiveness, frustration, bitterness, jealousy, envy, strife, and so much more. Once it has been handled, the love of God can begin to heal. God will bring peace, joy, hope, long-suffering, and kindness. Arrest sin and you can go free. That is why I keep saying to you drop the charges and you can go free!

Apostles, prophets, evangelists, pastors, and teachers — we are in a fight and we don't need any more games. So, stop playing them! It sounds good, but it is not good! Stop being shallow and give us the real Word of God! Cookies and candy taste good, but we can't live on them! It's time to get down to the real issues. Let's talk about what's killing the church, and that is sin! Yes, the forbidden word is in the bible, which God talked about quite often. Regardless of what we think, every now and then what the body needs is a good, old-fashioned rebuke!

Man up apostles, prophets, evangelists, pastors, and teachers. God gave you the charge to bring instruction and correction. Where are the leaders and the board of elders? The ones who will hold fast to the teachings of the Word of God and not worry about whether they will be called back to preach. Let's start giving the body of Christ some tough love.

My husband, at one point during his drug use, connected with a man in the city where we lived. This man was considered a recovering cocaine addict. They call it "recovery" in N.A.

(Narcotics Anonymous), but if we get it right in the house of God, then the cocaine addict can be delivered and won't need to be in recovery.

This man became his sponsor. So, on certain days I would take my husband to his sponsor's house. Again, I want to say if the church had the power of God operating in it the way that it should, I could have taken him to the church and the brothers at the ministry could have instructed or guided him. But the church was too busy fighting each other and talking about one another. Does this sound familiar?

So, one day — I will use "John" just to protect his identity — John met me at my car. We both knew that my husband was coming to the meetings, but was still smoking crack cocaine. He asked me, "Joyce, do you love your husband?"

My reply was, "Yes."

Then John goes on to say to me, "Then why are you loving him to death?"

I said, "Loving him to death? What do you mean?"

John told me that I was helping to kill him. "You are helping him self-destruct, because he can do his mess in the city and leave, and go to the country and not face the people he has wronged. He hides on the farm in the country. He never receives any consequences for his actions, so he continues to do the wrong things."

He told me to stop making it easy for him to escape his wrongdoings. Hold him accountable. Give him some tough love.

That is exactly what the church needs in these last hours — tough love. We have unspoken

I Didn't Come Here for This

issues, and things that we are afraid to talk about. Homosexuality, fornication, adultery, backbiters, liars, cheats, haters, bitterness, and unseemliness. It is like the Army's rule — don't ask, don't tell. If they look and act spiritual on Sundays and during any other service they come to, then take it for granted that they are spiritual. Don't worry about how they represent God on the job, how they live at home, and love and instruct their families. Forget about how they represent Him in the community, or anything outside of the hours of church. Don't worry about where they spend their Saturday nights and their ungodly lifestyles. Just hold them accountable for how they live and act on Sundays during church hours. Remember, don't ask, don't tell.

What are we thinking? The house of God is sick and we need help. We need to be told the truth about our mess. As a young child, I was always sick. And I hated all the nasty medicines, especially castor oil. I had a father who thought that castor oil cured everything. Even though I didn't like it, my parents believed it would make me feel better, so they gave it to me anyway. He would give it to me and make me eat a peppermint or some candy, which helped with the bad taste. But he still gave me the medicine because he knew I needed it. And guess what? It tasted really bad, but after taking it I would always feel better.

Which would you rather do? Give me what I need, or let me stay sick? Not only sick, but sick enough to die. One of the problems that we are facing in the body of Christ is the people who should be giving us the medicine can't because they are sick themselves. Ezekiel said, "Woe unto the shepherds that feed themselves and not my flock." ***Ezekiel 34:4 The diseased have ye not strengthened, neither have ye healed that which was sick, neither have ye bound up that which was broken, neither have ye brought again that which was driven away, neither have ye sought that which was lost; but with force and with cruelty have ye ruled them.*** God is going to judge His shepherds and He is going to hold you accountable for His people, because the shepherds refuse to give the body of Christ what it really needs.

Many are allowing the body to slowly die because the shepherds are loving it to death — just as I was doing to my husband. I was not holding him accountable; I was loving him to death.

The bible tells us that *the wages of sin is death,* but the gift of God is eternal life. We are accepting sin and the body is dying. Sin is living and we are dying. Wow! We need to hold the body of Christ accountable for the ungodly lifestyles that they live, from the pulpit to the door! Sin has crept into our sanctuary and it is alive and well, and we are sick and dying. People of God, what are we thinking about? Let's go to war and drive it out. It is an unwelcome guest!

Another thing hurting us is we are allowing the gifts and the hirelings to rule in the house of God, prostituting and pimping their callings, gifts, and talents. And, while I am on this subject, I want the entire body of leadership to take time to do some soul-searching right here. Are you guilty of allowing the gifts and talents to rule the order of the house of God? Accepting the gifts and talents and leadership of hirelings? Using them to try to usher us into God's presence? Are you guilty of knowingly compromising the standard of holiness? Allowing men and women whose lives do not represent a love for God or a lifestyle of godliness to lead us into God's presence?

Now, before you start writing your letters, I am not talking about every area of the church, because there is a business side to ministry. And in that area we do need trained and skilled persons with the appropriate knowledge to handle the business; especially with the laws we have today. But there is a difference between the two.

What I am saying is, when it comes to the holy things of God, we need men and women of God who are not perfect, but have a heart and a mind to live holy! Because there are some places in ministry that only the righteous can go! And as the body of Christ, it will take the righteous to lead us there — especially if we are going to be healed!

Because of the times that we live in, the gifts are being exploited. Not by persons who are shepherding their talents and gifts, but by hirelings. Real men and women of God will fight for the flock, but a hireling will leave the flock. We have hirelings that are taking advantage of their gifts in the body of Christ. They use them for selfish gain.

What we must understand is if they are not anointed of God, then they will never be able to lead us to a place where they themselves cannot go. We need true worshipers. Jesus told the Samaritan woman at the well that there will come a time when the true worshiper must worship in spirit and in truth. If we are going to grow, then our lifestyle has to become worship. And these are the people who can lead us — those who have made their lives worship.

What is a true worshiper? ***Psalm 24:3-6*** says it like this. ***Who shall ascend into the hill of the Lord? Or who shall stand in his holy place? [4] He that hath clean hands, and a pure heart; who hath not lifted up his soul unto vanity, nor sworn deceitfully. [5] He shall receive the blessing from the Lord, and righteousness from the God of his salvation. [6] This is the generation of them that seek him, that seek thy face, O Jacob. Selah.*** It is the generation that is seeking God. That is the generation that can lead us into His presence. It is the sons and daughters that have a love and a passion for the work of the Lord that can lead the Kingdom of God. It has nothing to do with talent, ability, or gifts.

We need leaders standing before us who have made their lives ones of worship. And without these examples before us, we leave our sanctuaries empty and hungry, still needing a word from the Lord.

The reason we are still hungry is because our hearts were not prepared through worship to receive the Word of the Lord. Prior to God speaking, we were ineffectively led through worship by ungodly people. These carnally minded men and women are not living in the will of God or accepting His grace, but are walking in sin. And because of sin, it is blocking the flow of God.

That is why, in reality, we are not being

seated down in His presence. The bible says, who can stand in His presence? Psalms says it like this: He who has clean hands and a pure heart. If our hands and hearts are not clean and pure, we cannot lead or even stand! I ask, where are the gifts of discerning spirits in the house of God? Who will tap into the heart of God and see the enemy through the eyes of God so that His people can be free to worship?

I will say it like this: Because the wrong people were leading us, we missed the Word of God. When the men and women of God began to speak, we could not hear what God was saying simply because our hearts were not prepared to receive. We had hirelings leading us, and they themselves couldn't go in, so they could not seat us in His presence. If the body of Christ is led by hirelings, we will never be able to enter as a whole into the Holy of Holies.

Pastors, you wonder why the message has not penetrated the hearts of the people of God. It is because we never got an opportunity to be seated in His presence and become quiet in our spirits. It is only when we have sincere and true worship leaders standing before us that we can be seated before Him. The real worshippers know how to settle us down and seat us in His presence. God has proven them by fire and they have paid the price to stand before Him.

As we know, there is a world full of gifts and talents, because gifts and callings are without repentance. Leaders, when we build with the wrong material, and when we build on the wrong foundation, it leaves the ministry weak and unstable. The gift begins to rule and direct the ministry, rather than the fivefold ministry (the Apostle, Prophet, Evangelist, Pastor, and Teacher).

This perverted foundation will never stand. And if it stands, it will never be able to support the weight of glory that God will desire to send in the house.

This leaves the ministry constantly wondering and walking in fear that the gifted persons will leave the ministry, manipulating their desire to gain control of the ministry and rule it with their gifts and abilities. Their stance is "we will leave if you don't nurse and yield to our every desire." And this is called witchcraft and the spirit of control. Many times they were never committed, anyway. How can they be committed to God's house if they are not committed to God?

Building ministries that have become gift-driven rather than apostle, prophet, evangelist, pastor, and teacher-established leaves the body sick and weak. Leaders, we as the children of God are crying, "Where are you?" and "When will you take a stand?" How long will you settle for the display of flesh in the sanctuary of God because it excites the people, leaving the body unequipped to handle the attacks of the enemy, as many are weak and unskillful in the Word of God? We are the light of the world. And if we, as the body of Christ, don't present to the world the genuine, bright light of God, then they will only see God dimly through us.

We need to give the people of God some tough love. Let's start holding each other accountable for the things we are doing wrong in the Kingdom. We have to get our heads out of the sand and stop acting like nothing is happening. We are self-destructing from the inside. We need to start in our pulpits and pews and end at the door, and hold each other accountable! The enemy has crippled us with fear, and this is hurting those who need to be saved. We must stand up and be the body of Christ that God will be pleased with.

Let's say a prayer:

Father, in the name of Jesus we come asking for forgiveness as Your sons and daughters. We are sorry that we have neglected to demonstrate to each other the love and the kindness that we should display. Forgive us for not becoming the examples of Godliness to a dying world that You have called us to be. Teach us, oh Lord, how to be sincere and to love each other. Let Your light shine in our hearts so much so that darkness will have to flee! Make us become the real church and Kingdom citizens that You shed Your blood for us to have the right to be.

God, thank You for taking away from us our selfish agendas and refocusing on the plan of salvation that is ahead of us. Now that we are here, give us ears to hear what You are saying to every believer, and the heart to receive Your Word, and the determination to never stop fighting until You come and receive us home. This is from Your loving and wounded sons and daughters. We love You, Father! And all these things we ask in the name of Jesus Christ.

Amen

Chapter Four
Somebody's Watching You!

*M*any times in our lives we take the simple things for granted, like the way we were raised, who our parents were, and the home training we received. We become so busy with life that we overlook the memories that we have with our sisters and brothers and our neighborhood friends. We become so carried away with the hustle and bustle of life that we very seldom go down memory lane.

If you take a close examination of your life, you will find that it is these experiences that helped to develop your character and your personality, whether they were good or bad. They made you who you are today.

Just think about it. It was the neighborhood bully that gave you the determination to never give up. He was the one who taught you how to fight. If it hadn't been for the bully continuously knocking you down, you would never have learned how to get back up. I don't know why God uses painful experiences to teach us valuable lessons, but He does.

Take the sensitive and compassionate friend who helped you believe you could win. Remember the one who was always there to encourage you when you failed? This friend helped you realize that there was a champion inside of you. What about the teacher who took the time to tell you that you mattered? Remember the little old lady who shared her wisdom so that you could learn to see a broader picture of life? It is these overlooked experiences that make you who you are.

Isn't it amazing that God uses all of these combined seasons of our lives? He uses the good as well as the bad to make us the people we are today. He uses everything about us, past and present, and gives us a passion or drive for our future to make us the individuals we have become. We would have never become who we are without the different people, places, and things we have experienced. Whether the people, places, and things were good or bad, they helped to form the way we see ourselves and the world that we live in. Everything is important and significant for God's plan in our lives.

When I was a young girl, things were very different. Sunday was a day that was committed to family and church. Many of the stores closed on Sundays because they considered it the Lord's day. I didn't grow up in an environment where my parents were super religious, but they did respect and have reverence for God. On Sundays you did not wash or do any type of work. Sunday was a day for family and rest, and my mother made sure of that.

My mother was a woman who made sure that we attended someone's church services on Sunday. She would get us ready for Sunday school even if she didn't go. Sundays were always considered a time set aside for God.

Although my mother and father were not overly religious, they taught me to have respect for God. When I think about not having a strict religious background, I sometimes wonder whether I would have been farther along with God than I am now if I had had a more formal religious background...or would that have taken me *farther away* from God? But nevertheless, God used all of these elements in my life to bring me to where I am today.

Even though I didn't have the foundation I thought I should have had spiritually, God knew just what to use to develop me into the woman of God that I am today. He knew what type of parents to give me. And what I can say is that my parents loved me in spite of all of their issues. Were they perfect? No. Did they always do the right things? No. But did they do the best that they could with the knowledge that they had? Absolutely, yes they did.

My mother was never seen kneeling and praying, but I knew that she would pray, because when she would be driving or cleaning or working she would talk to God. As a little girl, I would often ask her, "Who are you talking to?" and her reply would be, "God." It was kind of funny, because from nowhere she would begin to mumble words under her breath.

During those times it seemed like she had disconnected from her surroundings and it was Him and her alone. And every now and then she would let us in on the conversation, because a few words would slip out. She would always have an intense look on her face that let me know they were communing together, and I knew without a doubt that she was talking to Him. It's strange, but I find myself doing the same thing now. I was watching my mother.

My mother never made me attend prayer meetings. She didn't make me attend bible study regularly. I was not a pew baby and the majority of my time was not spent in the house of God with the singing, shouting, dancing, and the speaking in tongues. But what my mother did talk about was her faith in God. She would always say, "I asked God and He answered me."

So, I didn't learn to do church. I was not introduced to all of the church rules. I didn't learn the church vernacular or the church culture. What I did learn was to trust in God. When everything is falling apart, simply trust in God.

As a child, I didn't see many miracles. We were not in a ministry where they spoke in tongues (I stumbled into that later). No one was super spiritual and deep. I wasn't around prophets or prophetesses. But what I did see was a mother who believed in God.

What you may not understand is why I am telling you all of this. The reason I feel the way I do about God is because God didn't find me in my praise. God found me lost in my pain. I was not at the altar when God arrested my heart, I was in a car driving down a lonely highway by myself, hurting, rejected, and frustrated. I was totally broken by life. The pain of life was closing in on me and He was the only one who was revealing to me His infinite love.

I didn't have a secret prayer closet or church training; no scriptures to refer to. But what I did know was what my mother showed me. I could talk to God and He would answer. God would answer was all I knew. If the people who had turned their backs on me would not answer, I knew God would. My mother showed me a secret as a little girl. And that secret is...*God will answer.* How long He will take to answer and what He will say, I never know. But what I do know is that He answers every call. God will answer!

So, on I-75 South headed to Troy, Michigan, God and I had a conversation that changed my life forever. I said, "Lord, what's going on...and will You please help me?" I told Him that I was sorry, and please forgive me for hurting Him. I told Him that I wanted to live for Him for the rest of my life. It was that simple. And He answered me and saved me. That was twenty-two years ago and I meant it then as much as I mean it now. My desire is to live to please Him until I die.

I don't want to paint a picture of a perfect childhood, because we had some serious issues, but I survived. Don't get me wrong — my parents believed in God and respected Him, but they didn't always show us a reflection of godliness.

My father, on the other hand, was a man who spent his time (when he was not working) lying across the foot of his bed reading the bible. But he refused to attend church services on Sundays. He was the opposite — no church for him, but we would wake up on Sundays to all the gospel music we could stand. Songs like "I'm Climbing Up on the Rough Side of the Mountain" and "I'm Doing My Best to Make it in."

One of my father's favorite preachers was Pastor C.L. Franklin. He loved the message "The Eagle Stirs the Nest." Although, I think this message just might have been one of my dad's favorites, because we would wake to the smell of grits, bacon, biscuits, and eggs and he would dance around the kitchen and that was his church service. It was always so funny.

I would ask my father why he didn't attend church services with us, and his reply was, "God is too big to play with." He said that he was not ready to give up his tobacco and his alcohol, and he refused to go to church and act like he was living right. He said that he could become a deacon in the church if he wanted to, but he would not play with God.

Now that I am older, I respect my father's position because he wasn't trying to be something he was not. And he certainly was not a stumbling block for someone else. You knew where he stood in life and he would never pretend to be Godly or spiritual — or anything else, for that matter, that he was not. With him it was "what you see is what you get." My father taught me to be real. He was not a hypocrite.

There are a lot of things that I don't understand about life or God. But the things that I do understand I stand on. Life is just life, and it has a way of taking you around some bumpy and curvy roads. But one thing you can be certain of is that life is continuously changing and nothing stays the same — things that you don't expect, pain that you didn't anticipate — life happens whether we are ready for it or not. It happens whether we want it to or not. But what we must remember is that God is always in total control. Even when it looks like He is not, He is still in control. Even though you are waiting for greatness, but what you get in between is disappointment, continue to believe and make the best of it. Pick up the pieces and K.I.M. — Keep It Moving!

That is why, men and women of God, we have to be ready. Not because we are afraid that we won't make it to Heaven or we won't please God, but we have to be ready to give a reasonable answer of the hope that lies within us. There are people who come from different backgrounds and different cultures. They are full of pain and frustration. They don't understand God or His people, but they recognize that they need change. We have to be ready to point them in the right direction. And that direction is to Jesus Christ, our Lord.

We are the light that God is using to point the way. If our light is hidden, the world walks in darkness because we are the lights of the world. We are the lighthouses shining over the dark seas. When the storms are raging, we point the way to the shore. We light the way so that the masses don't run upon the rocks of life and become lost or destroyed.

But if our lights are dim, how can we point the way? By having a dim light or no light at all, look at the destruction it leaves. Who will light the way? That is why it grieves me when we are caught up in our own agendas. And if it grieves me and I am only human...think of what it does to God!

When I think about the people of God and the things that distract us from the work of the Lord, it blows my mind. Please don't get me wrong. I am not writing this because I desire to find fault in you, the reader. I am writing this because I see in my life the errors and the silly distractions and flaws in myself. How many times has the enemy caused me to get off course from the plan that God has for my life? More times than I want to count. I feel like I have wasted time, yet the conviction of God has caused me to challenge myself and others to find God's will and plan and walk in it. Someone is watching and waiting for me to get it right so they can believe that what I tell them about God is real. In actuality, they are depending on me to show them a life of holiness. And when I fail to do that, I misrepresent the Kingdom of God. So, it bothers me, especially when I see the pain it causes others because of my neglect.

That is why when I woke up this morning, I began to cry out to God to refocus us in the Kingdom of God. It upset me to the extent that I could not stop crying, and my heart was heavy. Don't get me wrong, I am guilty, too. Guilty as charged — but God knows I am crying every day, **"Lord Help Me!"**

Just thinking about people who are dying because they feel hopeless, and knowing that we have the answer, bothers me. We have a wonderful Father many of them know nothing about, and the reason for it is because we refuse to tell them. This breaks my heart. I lay before God and cried out to Him. I cried, "Lord, we are Your sheep and You are our Good Shepherd. We need Your help, Father. Please come and fix the mess that this world is in. Give us a heart and a mind to obey and Lord, **Keep us focused!"** Mother Potter tells me this all the time: "Stay focused, baby, stay focused! There is so much work to be done!"

Then, after crying out to God, to make matters worse, I got on the Internet and checked my Facebook page out. One of my friends on Facebook posted an article that really disturbed me even more. The article was about a mother who went to the Social Service Department and was denied assistance. She took a gun and held some of the employees hostage. After the police continued to talk to her, she released the employees and then she ended her life and shot her two children.

Can you imagine the devastation that her children and her family are left with? At the time it was not certain whether the children would survive. Who will be there to help them make sense of this painful experience without them becoming angry and bitter with God? If we are preoccupied and distracted with insignificant issues, it is the people who are really hurting that suffer.

This woman was dealing with a difficult place in her life and she had no one to help her through this tight place. And I thought, *We are in the church bickering over stupid stuff while the world is falling apart.* **Please God, Help Us!**

For some time now God has been giving me a reality check. And what I am beginning to realize is that God is forcing me to see the pain and the neglect of the world, and the consequences of sin. He is forcing me to look at the things we take for granted and the lack of concern for His people. While I was wasting time trying to be accepted and liked in the church, I was missing the real harvest in the world. I am now asking God to please redeem the time.

So, now I am glad that the church has rejected me more than once. It seems like I just don't fit in. And to be honest, I am not upset because I was never supposed to fit in. God has designed me to fit perfectly in the Kingdom of God. Hallelujah! I am a part of the church, which is His bride. But down here in the earth realm I operate on a Kingdom mentality. I don't see church, I see the Kingdom!

That is why I can place my heart and mind on how to heal and comfort hurting people everywhere. My heart and mind are set for changing not the church, but becoming a part of healing the nations and building God's Kingdom. I have left the local church mentality. Thank you, Jesus. I finally got the lesson. It took a lot of pain and suffering, but I got it. No more church as usual; it is all about the Kingdom.

And if that wasn't enough, I read another article on AOL about a twenty-three-year-old woman in Chicago who killed her three-month-old baby after partying and drinking all night. She then took the baby to the mall for seven hours and shopped.

I was telling this story to an Evangelist friend of mine, and she said to me, "Not only are they walking around in the mall with dead babies, but they are walking around in the church with *spiritually* dead babies." Wow! She said that we have people claiming to be spiritual parents and they have nothing to give these spiritual children, and these babies are spiritually dead. **Again, I say wow!** We have "dead" babies in the house of God, as well as outside the house of God.

Wake up! We are at war!

People of God, open your eyes and see the big picture. Our country's moral standards are decaying because we have lost sight of the concept of "in God we trust." But there is still hope, and we are the ones God has chosen to administer the healing.

2 Chron. 7:14 — If my people, which are called by my name, shall humble themselves, and pray, and seek my face, and turn from their wicked ways; then will I hear from Heaven, and will forgive their sin, and will heal their land. This verse is not a cliché. We have said it over and over. To some it may have become boring, and we might feel it is no longer original, but it is more alive today than it has ever been. It is time for God's people **to be humble, pray, seek,** and **turn**. And then God will heal. This scripture has not lost its power. If we take it to heart and apply it, it will work...*if we work it.*

People of God all over the world (not just in America), **it is praying time!** I am not writing only to Americans. I am writing to the churches all over the world. No, you don't have the same social issues as Americans, but the enemies that occupy your shores and regions are destroying your homeland security. And that security only comes through Christ Jesus. **The body of Christ is hurting everywhere!**

Can you see what we are facing inside and outside the house of God? We are living in evil and distressing times, and the church has its head in the sand arguing over insignificant issues. Let's break open our Pandora's boxes and get to the real issues so we can be healed in the house of God. Then and only then will we be in a position to give healing to others.

We have bigger and better churches, but both the quality of the people and the standard of holiness in these churches are weak. The buildings and the physical environment are great, but the character and commitment of the people toward God is small and unimportant. Many are committed to the pastor, the board, or the department that they serve in, but their hearts are not committed to God. Their lives bring with them no Godly fruit of repentance and the leaders are okay with it as long as they bring their tithes, offerings, and memberships. These individuals are service-driven and not God-driven. And it is sad that their leaders never hold them accountable for their ungodly lifestyles. There is no community fellowship or discipline to hold these people accountable to the standard of Godliness. When will we stop and truly seek the plan of God?

The bible tells us in *Psalm 127:1 — A Song of degrees for Solomon. Except the Lord build the house, they labour in vain that build it: except the Lord keep the city, the watchman waketh but in vain.* We have to learn how to stop building church edifices and ask God how to build Godly character in His people so that His Kingdom will grow and thrive. It is God who will give to us the blueprint to building His Kingdom. Leaders, will you please take a minute out of your busy schedule to ask God? Contrary to popular opinion, He really does know how it is done! When will we stop *doing* church and *become* the church?

I have never understood why many are doing church when God is about the Kingdom. And in a Kingdom you have all kinds of people. Yes, even those you like and dislike. Okay, I said it again; there are people in the Kingdom that we don't always like simply because they are different. And yes, there are people in the Kingdom that we think should look and act a certain way! Do they love God? Yes, of course. But they don't fit our description of holiness, so we judge them according to *our* standards and not *God's* standards. We judge them by their outward appearance and not the inward man of the heart. We group these innocent and Godly people together and misidentify them.

Then there are the ones in the house of God who look and act like sheep. They have the church vernacular and appearance down to the letter. And what we have done is judge them by their ability to adapt to the church culture. As sad as it may seem, we have mislabeled them, and in actuality these are the ones the bible calls "goats and wolves in sheep's clothing."

The goats among us come in and butt the sheep with their stubborn attitudes, insisting on having their own way at any cost. Then there are the wolves. They come in and terrify the sheep with their angry, hateful, bitter, and cunning attitudes, and neither the wolves nor the goats are willing to change. The goats and wolves continue to keep the body of Christ off balance. That is why it is imperative that we correctly classify those that are not of God.

What is hurting the Kingdom is we are misidentifying who they are. We label them sheep when they are wolves and goats. And as the body of Christ, we are allowing them entitlement to areas in ministry that they should never be entitled to. Stop placing them in authority positions over God's people. Don't allow these mean and evil people to be paraded before the body of believers, because they are hateful and nasty.

The reason we are giving them these rights is because we are viewing them as children of God when they are not. Understand me clearly, because we have misidentified them, and this gives them the ability to purposely hinder and destroy the work of God. And whether you want to believe it or not, these wolves and goats are stopping the sheep from receiving the Word of God and the plan of God for their lives because of their distractions.

These wolves and goats are sent into the Kingdom to destroy the vision and the purpose of God. Some are even sent to destroy the men and women of God. It is in their ungodly nature to tear things down; that is who and what they are. It is in their DNA because Satan is their father. This is why, while we are building, they are destroying. We cannot allow them the same Godly privileges as the sheep.

Yes, they are in the church, and to be honest they will always be among us. But just because they are with us we cannot afford to categorize them as Kingdom citizens when they are not. They display acts of ungodliness continuously with no signs of repentance, but we refuse to see them as who they are. It is only when they have displayed signs of repentance and they have permitted God to change their ungodly nature that they may be accepted and entrusted into the sheepfold.

Here is another thing that is killing us — and we really need to seek God for His help with this. This has done our leaders an injustice, because we have made little gods of many of them. Do not get me wrong — we are to give honor to whom honor is due, but there is a place where we cross the line. We praise them more than we praise God. We have to remember that God is a jealous God, and there is but one God. Should we obey and respect our leaders? Yes, yes, and yes. But we must not go to an extreme and exalt them above God!

And another thing...we are busy fighting over titles and positions. God forbid if we accidently forget to call you "Evangelist" or "Elder." And if we make that mistake, you leaders make us feel like we have committed high treason. Now, that's a problem. Yes, I say again, there is an amount of respect that every leader should receive, but when we take it to extremes, that is where the sin is.

What is up with the power plays in the house of God? We are all a part of the body and every part is greatly needed and respected. Even though I can't see my heart, let me try to live without it. It might be small and hidden, but I really need it. Everyone in the body of Christ is important — even the ones we think are insignificant. Okay, where is that found in scripture? *1 Cor. 12:22-25 — On the contrary, it is much truer that the members of the body which seem to be weaker are necessary; [23] and those members of the body which we deem less honorable, on these we bestow more abundant honor, and our less presentable members become much more presentable, [24] whereas our more presentable members have no need of it. But God has so composed the body, giving more abundant honor to that member which lacked, [25] so that there may be no division in the body, but that the members may have the same care for one another.* We are all in this together, but we have to begin to work as a team.

So, when we waste time fighting over things like "I didn't get a key to the church"... "You didn't call my name"... "Whose turn is it to clean the church?"... "The kitchen is dirty"... "They won't let me preach or pray"... "She walked past me and didn't speak"... "She rolled her eyes"... Give me a break! Church, are you for real? The world is dying and hurting. The world has a great platform for anyone who desires to be used, and it is waiting to hear your voice. You don't have to have a Sunday morning dais. Hit the streets and start preaching. **Get busy!**

How long are we going to allow the enemy to trip us up? It is time to come outside of the church buildings and fight the real enemy. We have tucked our tails and buried our heads in the sand, and are afraid to face the real issue...and that is a world gone wild! It appears that we have settled for our church cultures and a "don't rock the boat" mentality.

God is bigger than our local churches, and when we begin to see Him as such, we will expand our view of outreach. We will become creative and pliable to our approach to spreading the gospel rather than promoting the pastor or the church, and we will see the value and worth of the Kingdom.

We need to come outside of the four walls of our sanctuaries and minister to those who are hurting. And take our tailor-made suits off, put our briefcases down, leave our parallel bibles at home, and give the world a simple gospel. It is time for the church to stop and listen, and meet the people where they are. Meet them under every bridge and in every homeless shelter; meet them in the battered women's homes, and in the prisons. Engage them in the cancer treatment centers and all the places where we are not seen. Let's present to this world the only answer that will work, and that is a loving savior by the name of Jesus Christ.

And that being said, here is another thing we expect. We want people to come in already processed and ready for service, and they are not. What we fail to understand is that the fruit from the harvest comes in different varieties, and they are coming to the house of God with strange characteristics, personalities, styles, and looks.

Some are tattooed from head to toe, piercings everywhere; different hairstyles and colors; some clean and some dirty. Some are leaving the nightclubs and are too broken to go home and change. Many are walking out of the crack houses, tired from a three- or four-day run, looking for help.

They are coming to the house of God hoping to find a pleasant smile. They are searching for someone who can help them make sense of their pain. Then you have some who are mentally challenged and emotionally unstable. They are showing up in our sanctuaries and they have no relationship or commitment to God. Regardless of the way that they enter the house of God, they are all looking for Christ and His help. And it should be our purpose as the body of Christ to ensure that they find Him when they get to His house — and *not* the mess that is in it.

People of God, what are we prepared to offer them? I have gone to ministries and never received a friendly handshake — and God forbid a pleasant smile. No one ever asked me what I needed or what they could do for me while I was there. What I did get were looks like, "Who is she?" and "Why is she here?" People of God, we need to stop the madness, because somebody's watching you.

Let's say a prayer:

Father, in the name of Jesus we ask that You would redirect the body of Christ. Bring us to a place where we will have a heart to be concerned about the needs of the hurting souls that are searching for You. Pull us together and stop the division that is among us. Give us the wisdom to gather in the harvest of souls. Teach us how to care for them when they come into Your house. Let us not be more concerned about carnal things while missing the spiritual opportunities to heal and minister to those who are hurting. We repent for our sinful and selfish behaviors and ask You to clean our hearts, minds, bodies, and souls for the work of Your Kingdom. Let us become more conscious of the needs of others

more than ourselves. Teach us, Lord, unity and love in Your house. We need Your clear direction and guidance. We are hurting and wounded, and Lord, we need You now! Send Your ministering spirits to help us and let Your presence change us. Give us the true heart of a servant. Thank You, Lord, because You are our Father and Friend.

These things we ask in Your son Jesus' name.

Amen

Chapter Five
Guilty as Charged and Here is the Evidence!

I would like to ask you, the reader, this: What is causing the fiber of our society to suffer from such a great level of decay and decline in morality? We are facing social issues that many have never imagined we would ever experience; things like homicide, sexual exploitation, child abuse, greed...and that is only to name a few. Everything we see and do is over the top. It is not done in small quantities; it is done in mass quantities. The world as we know it is in big trouble, and the generations to come will be left to clean up the mess. I want to ask you how we are supposed to fix the mess we are in, because there has to be a turning point.

After giving it some thought, I have come to the conclusion that no matter how we perceive the world, the system, our families, or our churches, there is an underlying cause for the declining condition of our society. We need to find out what is causing the bitter, hateful, and unforgiving nature of our loved ones and this world. We must become diligent in seeking answers so we can successfully impact, through change, the state of our culture. That is when we will be forced to take off our rose-colored glasses and see it for what it is. We must clearly define not our behavior, but the things that cause us to have the behavior we have.

We must look for and look at the most
overlooked thing of our own personal nature, and
that nature is sin. If we clearly look, we will
identify and trace the root cause right back to sin.
And from identifying the root cause as sin, we then
will receive a greater understanding of the deadly
fruits that sin produces. The fruits of sin are the
symbol of the ungodly behavior that we possess.

I understand that there are many different
things that displease God. And any of these sinful
natures that we battle with have greater or lesser
degrees. But the main issue is they cause a dividing
line between us and God. If I dealt with all the sin
it would take volumes of books, and we would still
not do it justice. But in this chapter, I want to talk
to you about the thing that was killing me. This sin
starts out unnoticed, but when it matures it can be
very deadly.

It is the sin of unforgiveness. Unforgiveness
starts out very small, but grows out of control. It
causes decay in relationships, and it can be the
result of some of our sicknesses, and mental and
emotional disorders. Unforgiveness starts out as an
offense that the person refuses to apply grace to.

When we don't learn to forgive, we stand in
the spirit of pride and the seat of self-
righteousness. We refuse to give to others the one
thing that God so freely has given to us. We act as
if the grace of God has not been applied to our lives.
We pride ourselves in holding on to the offenses
and failures of others, while appearing self-
righteous to ourselves. We form the attitude of
being supreme. And for those who continue to hold
on to the spirit of unforgiveness, I want to ask a

question: Are you for real? Have you not needed forgiveness?

Whether you know it or not, it is during these times of self-righteousness that you are positioning yourselves as judge, jury, and executioner. This limits us from extending to our offender the mercy that God extended to us. The person or persons refuse to freely give the offender the grace of forgiveness. It is a known fact that any time you stand in the position of self-righteousness you are standing outside of the will of God.

I remember a time in my marriage when my husband had really hurt me with his actions. I can't, at this time, totally remember what he did, because I have forgiven him and forgotten about it. And now, when I talk about some of the things that he did, they are not as painful as before…but some are really funny.

Although I don't remember what caused it, I clearly remember my response to what he did. Whatever the offense was, it really frustrated me and made me very angry. And because of it, it caused great pain.

I can remember being at work and being angry. I sat down at my work station and was preparing to read the Word of God. Before I opened my bible I asked God what He wanted me to read. Because of the pain that my husband had caused me, I had purposed in my heart to get out of my marriage. I was at the point where I felt I'd had enough. This was "the straw that broke the camel's back" as we say.

So, trying to forget the pain and anger of my circumstance, I wanted to find answers in God's

Word. The funny thing now, when I think about it, is the answer that I wanted from God was not the answer that God wanted me to have. I wanted to hear what my flesh wanted, but God had an answer that would heal a hurting heart.

After asking God what to read that day, He gave me the scriptures in *Matthew 6:14-15 — ...for if ye forgive men their trespasses, your heavenly Father will also forgive you: [15] But if ye forgive not men their trespasses, neither will your Father forgive your trespasses.* Boy, I did not want to hear that. I can remember so clearly closing my bible and telling God, "I don't want to hear this today. I have made up my mind and I am divorcing him."

Then, after not reading the Word of God all day, and all the while planning what I needed to do to make my exodus from the marriage, I got into my vehicle and started home to have it out with my husband. I told myself all day, "It is over, and I ain't forgiving nobody! No, Lord, I don't care what You say!"

While I was driving home, I began to listen to a local gospel station on the radio. And when I pulled up in front of my house to get the mail out of the mailbox, the announcer said, "The scripture for the day is *Matthew 6:14-15 — For if ye forgive men their trespasses, your heavenly Father will also forgive you: [15] But if ye forgive not men their trespasses, neither will your Father forgive your trespasses.* Me being the me that I am, I turned off the radio and said again, "Lord, I still don't want to hear this. I don't care. He is out of here."

What I didn't realize then was how much God loved me. My loving Father understood that it was not my husband who was suffering — it was me. The offense was done and could not be undone even if my husband wanted to undo it. It was impossible to change what had happened. But what could be changed was the outcome of the effects from the pain that it had caused.

At that moment I had a choice to make. I could die with the pain from the offense, or be released from it by applying forgiveness. What God knew was that by extending forgiveness to others, it allows you to walk free of the burden of the offense. You have only two choices you can make; you can refuse to live with the offense through forgiveness, or you can choose to be tied to the offense by unforgiveness.

If you choose the latter, then you have chosen a life of emotional imprisonment. The offense becomes your canvas of pain to view until you desire a change of scenery. The offender cannot make this choice for you — it is up to you to choose it for yourself. It is a gift that you give to yourself.

When dealing with unforgiveness, you become the judge, the warden, the guard, and the prisoner all at the same time. You are the one who walks you to the jail cell, and it is you who slams the door behind you. Unfortunately, you also determine how long the sentence will be. And while you are there, you run the facility. It is your behavior that determines how the external and internal conditions will be affected. If you choose to hold on to unforgiveness, it is at that point you set the atmosphere of defeat for the remainder of your sentence because of the offense. The sad part about it is, if you don't release it, a short jail sentence can turn into a death sentence.

Can't you see the picture that was being painted that day with my husband? I was facing life imprisonment, or even a death sentence, and didn't know it. God understands everything about us. He knew that I had been caught in a trap, and if left there I would die. That's why God was instructing me.

But because of the pain that I was in, I still refused to listen to God speaking to me at my mailbox or on my job. Although I wouldn't listen to God, He continued to talk — and that is the thing I love about this story. The love of God refused to allow me to stay in the pain that I was in, because He knew that if I stayed in that condition, I was looking to serve an emotional prison sentence. And the sad part about it was that I was the one making the arrest!

But the God that we serve is so awesome. Later that evening, I went to our Wednesday night bible study. My pastor was doing a series on financial freedom. But he stated that while he was studying for the class, the Lord spoke to him and told him to change the bible study for that night. I am sure you can guess what the bible study was all about. His lesson was on the power of forgiveness and what unforgiveness does to us. I was very quiet and reserved. In the middle of his lesson he looked at me and said, "Sister Hawkins, you are not saying anything."

At that point God had broken through the stony part of my heart. I began to cry. It was in that bible study that I finally released my pain from the offense and surrendered to the will of God.

So, if you see unforgiveness from the surface it might appear to be insignificant, but it grows and manufactures other types of fruit. Unforgiveness, if left unchecked, will turn into anger; then anger into bitterness; then bitterness transforms into hatred. And hatred evolves into rage, and rage into suicide or murder.

Look at the path of destruction that unforgiveness leaves. It starts out with an offense that you refuse to let go of. Then, because you won't release it, you become angry. Then you hold on to the anger for so long that it becomes part of your nature. So, rather than dealing with unforgiveness at the beginning, you have now allowed it to settle into your spirit and your heart. Then anger leads to bitterness. Now you are associating everything with the thoughts or the acts of resentment caused by the person who offended you, and that causes you to become bitter. You find yourself not seeking good in anything that the offender says or does. Unforgiveness is so cruel that, if not addressed immediately, before you realize it not only will you be fighting unforgiveness and bitterness, but the two walk hand and hand with jealousy. Look at what a mess unforgiveness causes.

Then you have to consider that if bitterness goes unchecked, it will grow into hatred. At that point you have moved from unforgiveness and bitterness, accompanied by jealousy, into hatred. You find yourself having an extreme dislike for the offenders. You can't stand to hear their names. You despise seeing them. Anything that represents them causes you anger, envy, and disgust. Just the mention of their names emotionally disrupts everything within you. Now the prison you are in is closing in around you even more.

If you pass by the opportunity to challenge hatred and not attempt to get rid of it, you are left to battle the spirits of rage, suicide, or murder. Now you are not satisfied with shunning or looking down on the offender; your desire is to see them suffer for the offense.

And if the offender cannot be touched emotionally or physically, then you turn your pain inward to self-destruct, which is suicide. This person or persons not addressing these feelings or emotions will begin to set out to destroy the offender or themselves, because the fruit of hatred matures into rage, suicide, or murder.

You begin to kill that person with your mouth. You assassinate their name or their character. You plot lies and falsely accuse them of things they had no part in. You try to destroy their character and influence. Rage and murder are very extreme emotions and can cause one to attempt to physically destroy the individual or the individuals who offended them.

Then there are times when the person who has been wounded cannot process their pain from the offense or the offender, and they turn their pain, anger, bitterness, unforgiveness, and rage inward and begin to self-destruct and commit suicide. I believe that unforgiveness can be one of the root causes of many addictions. Let me talk about me.

The place of pain in my relationship with my

husband, my family, my babies' daddies and just a series of painful events caused me to self-destruct. In reality, there were two people in the house trying to escape from their reality — me and my husband.

While my husband headed to the drug house, I headed to the refrigerator and the cookie jar. Oreo cookies eased my pain and became my comfort food. This is what I call real talk. I am just keeping it real and telling the truth, because these are facts that no one really wants to deal with.

We want to appear from the outside as though we have it all together, yet on the inside we are falling apart. I want to keep it real. It was not God I was looking for when I was in pain at those moments, it was relief. And during those times I never stopped to think that if I sought God and forgiveness, I wouldn't need to be soothed by food.

Can't you see the clear picture? If it was God I was searching for to give me comfort, then I would not have been reaching for the foods that pacified my pain. I hid behind food. It was too painful to deal with the issues that I was facing, so my escape was found in food. I was giving myself a death sentence that would be carried out slowly.

If I could have found a healthy way to process my pain and release my offender with forgiveness, I would have been released from my pain. But instead, I held on to the anger and chose to self-medicate with food, which caused me to feel a sense of comfort and entitlement. I felt that I was entitled to be angry and unforgiving; after all, it was me that they hurt. Not realizing that hurting people hurt other people, my husband and I were in a never-ending circle. I hurt him and he hurt me. Wow!

That is why I said that the method of suicide can be in any form of addiction, illness, lethal or emotional, and so many other ways to end it all and escape the reality of the pain. Just think — it all started with an offense and not having the capacity to forgive.

That is why we have to learn to quickly drop the charges so that we can have the liberty of freedom and be emotionally stable. You must take into consideration that all of the things I have spoken about and the power of these sins can be deadly. And if unattended, it can lead to decay and destruction.

So, now I pose a question to the body of Christ: How long are we willing to sit and watch the moral fiber of our families and society decay before we consciously and earnestly seek the help of God? It is God who heals and gives us the ability to apply forgiveness.

When we look at how simple the concept of forgiveness can be, we can see the peace and healing that it will bring to every area of our lives. But we have allowed our pride to cause forgiveness to slip out of our reach, and we have made it appear complex.

Many of our relationships have dissolved because we have not made forgiveness the fiber that holds them together. It is as though we have settled and accepted the defeat. We have allowed our pride, which God hates, to place us in a stalemate. And because of it, no one is winning. Look at what pride can and will do.

Because of unforgiveness and pride, we have settled to see our relationships with our loved ones and our communities die. That is why God hates it. He hates it and the destruction that it causes. God hates pride so much that He said He even hated a proud look. Isn't it sad that pride and unforgiveness cause us to hold on to things that we should have released?

Even in our churches we have allowed the spirit of unforgiveness, accompanied by pride, to reign supreme as a part of our worship experience in the body of Christ. These two spirits have poisoned our fellowship with one another. And because of it, our churches are lying immobile, and our communities have become war zones. We, as the body of Christ, are watching the world and our families fall apart.

We have not demanded that individuals in the body of Christ completely forgive one another, or hold them accountable because of their actions of unforgiveness. We, as leaders, have allowed them to parade before the body of Christ with their bitter and hateful lifestyles and misrepresent the Kingdom of God. That is why many of our ministries have started to decay. We have settled to receive these individuals' financial and gifting support rather than demand that they have a chaste and Godly conduct. Because of this, many ministries have lost their sense of mobility and have accepted this position of defeat.

Don't you see? If we, as a body of believers, are ever going to survive the state that we are in, we must have a move of God. And one of the things that limits this move is unforgiveness. What we must understand is when there is unforgiveness, it causes a loss of mobility in the spirit, and because of a lack of movement, this position becomes a very uncomfortable place. That is why the house of God is not finding the peace that it should have.

We have to deal with unforgiveness because it is causing us to stand still, and we are not receiving the harvest we should receive because we are not moving. We have lost our ability to move according to the will of God and by the power of the Holy Ghost.

And by being immobile, you are left in a position of pressured, non-purposeful movement, just as a patient would lie in a weakened, convalescent state. This convalescent state limits the individual's ability to meet their personal needs, or assist in meeting the needs of others. In other words, you are not going anywhere and are totally unable to reposition yourself.

Sisters and brothers in the house of God, we are stuck. And being stuck in this position causes great pain. Unforgiveness has caused us to become stagnant not only in the house of God, but in every relationship that we are in.

That is why many times you might be sitting in a peaceful environment and think of something you thought you had forgotten about. And just the *thought* of the event will cause you pain, and you will allow that pain to negatively affect the peaceful environment you are in.

That is why many of us suffer with trust issues — we have not allowed God to heal us from the past pain of unforgiveness. The sad part is that you may have forgiven the other person, but did not forgive yourself. You are left stuck in a cycle of pain and frustration...all because of unforgiveness and its effects. Because of unforgiveness, you have now switched roles and you have become the offender. My friend, what is happening is, since you are not willing to release the pain or allow anyone else to help you with the pain — no, not even God! — you find yourself taking out your pain, frustration, and hurt on good and wonderful people who only want to love you.

God help us, please! Don't get me wrong, this book is healing me as well as you. I am looking at the woman in the mirror and I am asking her to change her ways. There is real and true healing for the body of Christ — we just have to ask God for it. There is also healing for the sinner. You just have to seek after it.

Another thing about being in a convalescent position is it leaves you unable to attend to your needs, because you are lacking the ability to effectively use your limbs. Can't you see that this is what the house of God is beginning to look like? All of our members are not functioning well. They can't move. We look like convalescents.

The different parts of the body of Christ have become immobile and not able to fitly supply all of the needs. We have become ineffective in doing the work of the Lord, and the reason is we are overworking the healthy parts of the body, because the unhealthy parts either can't move or refuse to move and function according to the will of God.

Those members not willing to move in the flow of the Holy Spirit or follow after God are drying up and withering away, leaving the extra burden on the healthy members.

The body of Christ is being pulled in so many different directions that it is leaving the sick and spiritually immobile members suffering from a lack of attention. And because of their immobility and convalescent state, they are left suffering and spreading diseases to other areas of the body. And the reason for this is because no one is there to give them the attention or healing that they need from the Word of God, or they refuse to accept the help.

Because the body of Christ is ineffectively ministering to these people, and these spiritually diseased members are being left unattended, it gives them an opportunity to spread gossip, lies, hatred, and distrust. You will find that many of them have no respect or love for each other or their leaders. Also, because they are being left spiritually sick, you find them poisoning other healthy members and causing them to become weak. It is all because these individuals refuse to be delivered through the blood of Jesus Christ, or hear the sound of the Kingdom of Heaven. This leaves the body of Christ left suffering from poor circulation issues in the anointing of God. My God, my God, my God!

Leaders, it is up to you to ensure that the body of Christ is healthy and secure. When you neglect to take care of or exercise and move these parts of the body of Christ, and demand spiritual therapy for them, they begin to break down and lose their use and eventually require amputation.

Leaders, you are the therapists that God desires to use. He has trained and equipped you to exercise and strengthen us. If we fail, it is because you have failed both us and God. Stand up and trust God and do your job, even if it hurts you and us. We may weep, moan, and cry, but in the long run we will heal. Don't stop because of the pressure. If we are to be healed, we, as the body of Christ, must endure the pain.

My sisters and my brothers, because we are in such a convalescent state, the body of Christ is breaking down right in front of our eyes. But if we die, it is because of us, because God has given us the answers in His Word.

Leaders, it is because of your lack of care. You have shifted and changed the truth of God, and refused to hold us accountable to the Word of God! Preach the Word and nothing but the Word. It is the pure Word of God that will heal us! That is why we are hurting and we can't do anything about it. There are sin issues in the church that no one wants to address or deal with. And because of it, we are beginning to break down.

Anytime you become spiritually immobile, you are subject to receive deep, gaping wounds, and it will also leave painful sores. The immobility will cause the tissues to become unhealthy and break down. That is why we are hurting so. The body of Christ is in pain. Let's deal with the real issue — and that issue is sin!

The sad part is if sin is left unattended, and we stay in this position without prompt attention, it can and will lead to death. My God — what are we doing, church? We are hurting and we are dying slowly. We must get the entire body healed and whole so that those who are lost will find a healthy environment to come to and receive their healing.

If we are sick on the inside, how can we have the strength to heal those on the outside? That is why the sinner settles for finding more comfort on the outside of the church — because of the things they hear going on inside of the church. Isn't it sad to know that the unbeliever feels that they can't trust the place where they should be able to come and be healed?

We are wounding them in the house of God, and they have never even come into our sanctuaries. It is so heartbreaking to think that they are afraid to come and see what we have to offer. They see how we represent God outside of His house and they refuse to come into the house to find out about Him. Our conduct is terrible!

That is why we are missing the sinner, because of the way we act. There are real, hurting people who are seeking for God, and we have grossly mishandled them. Church, we cannot afford to miss this season! We have to be prepared for them when they reach the house of God so they can be healed, delivered, and set free.

But how can we handle the harvest of souls when we are having a hard time dealing with each other? We are bickering and fighting with one another. These men and women are coming to the house of God looking to be healed and learn more about God, but what they are not prepared for is the war zone that we offer them. Then we have the nerve to say that what we are doing is "friendly fire." We declare, "I love my sisters and brothers in the Lord," all the while killing each other at the same time. How can sweet and bitter water come from the same fountain? What in the world does hurting each other have to do with being friendly? Where is simple holiness in God's house?

I ask you, how can we cope with all of their dissimilarities and indiscretions when we have so many ourselves, and then in turn provide a somewhat peaceful place for fellowship and worship?

If we are honest, there is too much drama in the church! The church is hurting and we can't quite figure out how to get it to stop. Not only is the church hurting, but it is hurting the people that it should be healing — especially the potential convert. As I said before, hurting people hurt other people.

Why are we hurting? As I have said so many times, it is because we refuse to forgive. What we must understand is the ability to forgive is not an easy thing to do. To forgive takes a conscious effort. You have to purposely make an effort to apply it to the person who has hurt or offended you. It requires that you look past the pain of the act and see a greater outcome for yourself and the person you choose to forgive.

As the body of believers, we are holding on to things that we should have completely let go of. We are guilty as charged, and there is a lot of evidence to prove it.

I think this will be a good place to pray:

Father, in the name of Jesus, we are hurting — and because we are hurting we are causing other people to hurt. Lord, heal us of our past pain and disappointments. Give us the strength to forgive those that have wounded and offended us. Show us how to apply forgiveness as You have commanded of us to do in Your Word. Teach us to love those who have spitefully misused us. Take the bitter seeds of unforgiveness far away from us and fill our hearts with love. Cause Your peace to settle within us and heal our minds and souls. Allow us to forget the offenses, and if we remember them, let us not remember the pain that they bring. Let us show the spirit of compassion to our offender and let them see us giving to them the gift of forgiveness that You gave to us. Let them see the love that we have for You displayed in us. Let us be the example to others as You have been an example to us. Teach us to symbolize the power of love that You have revealed to us through Your son, Jesus Christ. He was the perfect example of what forgiveness should represent. It was because He gave His life for His enemies that we have the power to do the same for our enemies. We trust and love You, Lord. These things we ask in Your son Jesus' name...

Amen

Chapter Six
He Healed the Little Girl in Me

*I*n this book my assignment is to paint a clear picture of the power of this evil spirit, which is the spirit of unforgiveness. It has stripped, robbed, and destroyed families, ministries, businesses, and even nations from having great relationships because of an offense. Unforgiveness has crushed every type of relationship that can exist. This spirit of unforgiveness is so bad that it will cause you to solicit people to uphold your views and your reasoning for holding on to your bitterness and your anger. It will give you a support system to nurture your pain, frustration, and disappointment.

You know the friends you call to help you prove your point of how you've been hurt? Remember the ones who will help you wallow in your pain, never looking for a place to make sense of the situation or to bring peace to it; the people who will not help you find peace between you and the offender, or peace within yourself? The ones who say, "Yeah, girl, I wouldn't take that if I were you." The person who will remind you that you deserve better, and you should have nothing else to do with them. "They should not have hurt you like that, and I wouldn't give them a second chance."

What you don't understand is what they are really saying is, don't look for a reason to forgive them. Hold on to your bitterness — it's okay. Make it your best friend. It will keep you company every day of your life. It will never let you forget. And even after the relationship is over, you can transfer your pain to every relationship thereafter, causing each relationship to suffer and die because of your pain.

Yes, the pain that you refuse to let go of, my sisters and brothers, can and will be lethal. I want you to know that this spirit of unforgiveness is brutal. It will leave you alone with your pain to suffer and die slowly. Sadly enough, its strategy is to keep you preoccupied for the rest of your life with an over-stayed memory of guilt and frustration. It supplies you with a recording of the offender and a play-by-play of the offense. Unforgiveness also makes sure that you have enough evidence and clues to lead you to a trail of anger, bitterness, and then hatred. Unforgiveness destroys the very essence of who you are and who you are to become. It is a cruel adversary.

This spirit keeps you preoccupied with unimportant issues rather than have you focus on the things that really matter. That is why, in the house of God, we are still holding on to the things that we should have overcome and forgotten about, preventing us from moving forward. If we are not careful, our messages and ministries can become a reflection of what we refuse to let go of. Have you ever sat in service and heard the pain of the speaker leaking forth in the totality of their discourse? Their message sounds like the pain that they continue to cling to. That is what unforgiveness will do. You will find yourself sounding like your pain.

That is why it is important to let things go

quickly. The bible tells us not to waste even a day holding on to something that causes you to become angry. It says don't let the sun go down on your wrath, because God knows that the longer you hold on to the offense, the deeper the wound becomes. And what would have been a short process has now become a greater task to overcome. But when you quickly give it over to God, the sooner the healing can begin.

Holding on to the offense allows you to feel a sense of entitlement to the pain and anger that it causes. This, in the long run, can become very destructive. Unforgiveness can take on a nature of its own. It wants to stay longer than needed, and when challenged, it will cause you to immediately look for a reason to justify your acts of unforgiveness, with statements such as "they had no right to treat me that way" and "I will never forgive them" or "I did not deserve what they did."

When the disciples asked Jesus to teach them how to pray, Jesus did not neglect to include in the prayer that they were to forgive. Jesus clearly taught them to ask God to forgive them of their transgressions just as they forgave others of their transgressions. Not only do we want God to forgive us, we want Him to give us the ability and the grace to forgive others.

Then Jesus took it a step further by telling us if we will not forgive others of their transgressions, our Father in Heaven will not forgive ours. That is why, on the subject of forgiveness, Jesus didn't leave a stone unturned.

Not only did He say forgive, but He taught us how often. Jesus said to the disciples to do it "seven times seventy in one day." He was letting us know that no matter how many times they offend you, you have to be willing to forgive. We have to drop the charges in the house of God. We have to offer forgiveness in our families, in our communities, and on our jobs, and especially in the house of God, so that the body of Christ can go free and do the work that the Lord has assigned us to do.

We are trying to set the sinner free in the house of God when we are locked up ourselves. Yes, many are set free from addictions, nightclubs, ungodly relationships, fornication and adultery, lust, and the sin of the flesh. And I say "many" because some are still fighting to gain victory. But it appears that we are not fighting the spirit of unforgiveness, jealousy, envy, gossip, strife, and division, and all these are byproducts of unforgiveness.

So, when you look closely at the big picture, unforgiveness has us imprisoned and we are not trying to break free. It is like cancer. It spreads and kills everything it comes in contact with. Can't you see the weak places that we must strengthen? Because, my sisters and brothers, the one foundational principle that we should be freely able to offer the sinner is a glimpse of forgiveness, and reveal to them its power. That is one of the foundational principles of the gospel. The gospel is about a loving savior who forgave His enemies.

And if we can't offer the sinner a clear picture of what forgiveness is, then we are missing the whole message of the gospel, because forgiveness is nothing but God's grace. I want you to know that when we are not willing to give others the same grace that God has given us, we are telling the sinner and unbeliever that the gospel has nothing to offer them. And you and I know that this is not true! The liberty of forgiveness is only given through the cross of Calvary and our savior, Jesus Christ. And whether you know it or not, forgiveness is a principal key to the very gospel that we teach and preach.

Oftentimes when a person is struggling with unforgiveness, they are not only struggling with forgiving others, but they are fighting with forgiving themselves. And the fact of the matter is because they have not applied the principle of forgiveness appropriately to their own lives, they become the victims of their own pain and they themselves suffer a great defeat. That is why many individuals, because they are not willing to forgive, struggle with one question, and that question is: How can God forgive me, because I don't know how to forgive?

What is the foundation of forgiveness? The foundation is that you have to make a choice to say, "I am letting it go." The decision is totally yours. When you choose to hold on to the offense, it causes you to struggle with the principle of forgiveness, and many times it's because you have not yet learned to forgive.

As ordinary people striving to live healthy and productive lives, we must learn to tell ourselves that we are better than what we have been through. So, since we are better than our painful experiences, we must be willing to let it all go and forgive. We must tell ourselves that we will not allow our offender to monopolize our time, our day, our energy, or our emotions. We must clearly understand the power of forgiveness and the cruelty of unforgiveness.

One of the greatest pictures that we must grasp and never fail to display is how forgiveness can effectively change and make better any painful situation. If we, as believers, cannot get this generation to conform to the power that this one principle of forgiveness holds, then we can expect to lose the generations to come. As believers of Jesus Christ, if we don't teach our sons and daughters by showing them the power that forgiveness holds, then all of our preaching and teaching is in vain.

We must closely look at the purpose of the work of Jesus Christ and find that He displayed the greatest act of forgiveness by redeeming all of mankind. And if we cannot learn to follow His example, we leave a misrepresentation of the cross. And if we leave this an open issue, we are leaving other generations a legacy that will say that the love that Christ had for all of mankind would have come without power. And we all know that this is also not true. Jesus' act of redemption came with great power, and that power is love and forgiveness.

As long as we lack the capacity to forgive, we will continue to be weak and sickly in the body of Christ because of the sin that is within us. But the thing I love about applying forgiveness is it gives us power and strength. **Lord, please have mercy!** It was only through God's forgiveness that we were set free.

There is another thing that I take issue with

in the body of Christ, and that is the fact that we desire to set the sinner free when we are in bondage ourselves in the house of God. We tend to believe that it is only the sinners who need to be set free. If we look closely, we will note that it is not only the sinners who need freedom, but also the people of God who need the freedom of Christ. It is only when we are free from our own indiscretions in Christ that we will possess the freedom and power to set the sinners free.

Although it is the sinners who need to see the true gospel revealed, we, as believers, need to be reminded that we are hurting ourselves and anyone we come in contact with if we have not effectively been released from our pain of unforgiveness. Can't you see the most painful thing is that the unbelievers are watching us self-destruct from the outside? Many of them are saying, "I have enough drama in my life. I don't need to come to church and have more." They are saying these things because they are seeing us fighting on the inside of our local assemblies, and they are the ones suffering the most because they are left without the gospel.

I have a niece who posted on her Facebook page a statement that bothered me to a certain extent. She said, "I like God, but I am not happy with His fan club." Guess who the fan club is? It is the believers. We are the fan club.

Isn't it amazing that we say we love Him, but misrepresent Him? Wake up, church! We are in big trouble. Not only are we hurting those who need Him — we are hurting each other!

Let's explore something else. If we are going

to work on healing the church, there is no way that it can happen without successfully administering healing to the family. The church is falling apart because the family structure at home is chaotic.

And the same thing that has crippled our ministries is crippling our family structure — and that is unforgiveness. When I forgave my husband, I saw everything in my life change. Forgiveness changed my health, my emotions, and my relationship with God. It allowed me to see God from a clearer and crisper view. I was able to see His compassion, long-suffering, meekness, and gentleness. The cloud of anger and chaos lifted and the peace of God entered. My pattern of self-destruction turned into my passion for loving and living my life in peace. All of my desires for life are transformed, and now I enjoy life. No matter what disappointment comes my way, I still see God at the center of it all.

I know some of you might be saying, "I cannot go back and have the same physical relationship with the people who hurt me." What you must understand is that forgiveness and trust are two separate issues. So, in some instances you are right, because forgiveness is a heart issue more than anything else. Forgiveness reaches into your heart and changes the way you see or relate to the individual or individuals who hurt, offended, or even violated you. It releases you from being a victim and places you in a place of victory.

Unforgiveness is like a weight full of pain and pressure that causes you to continuously defend or justify why you even have the right to be angry. Can you imagine waking up every day, replaying the incident, and finding a reason to stay angry — then feeling justified? Look at the unnecessary burden that unforgiveness causes you to carry.

Let me tell you a story about me. I was very sick and fighting for my life. The disease I had was killing me. Although the most painful thing and most obvious thing I was going through was my marriage, the fact that my husband and I were separated and preparing to divorce didn't help any. I was on my bedroom floor crying out to God for help. And the Lord began to talk to me about my second grade teacher.

I want to bring some clarity to this picture. At the time that we had this conversation, I was about forty-three years old, and God was confronting me about a second grade teacher. You know, I was thinking, *Why is He talking to me about this at this time?* It didn't make sense. I was going through hell. It was one of the worst times of my life.

The last thing I wanted to hear was something about a second grade teacher, especially when I hadn't been in school for ages. She was not my primary concern at that time. Surviving was. My thoughts were, *Lord, let's stay focused and deal with the issues at hand.*

Let me make this picture really clear for you. What I want you to understand is that I was lying in a pool of tears, weeping at the altar of God. I was having a complete emotional meltdown. I was losing it! So, why was He even mentioning my teacher? It didn't make a lot of sense when my family and health was falling apart. But God knew.

That is the unique thing I love about God. He knows how to get to the heart of the matter. He is so skillful in what He does that He does not leave any stones unturned. Even when we can't identify our pain, He knows what is hurting us the most.

Before He could deal with the present issues, He had to dig out the thing that was buried so deep that I thought I had forgotten it. After all, this seed of unforgiveness had become the pattern that taught me how to apply unforgiveness to every area of my life in the first place. This long-lasting bitterness had helped me identify whenever I thought someone would hurt me. It caused me to build unnecessary walls to keep good people out, just in case I thought they would hurt me. I had a defense mechanism for everyone I came in contact with, and guess how I learned to use it? You got it — my second grade teacher.

God had to break all of the chains that had been deeply hidden and had caused me to unconsciously decide to live with the pain and its effects. He couldn't release me from the obvious bondage until the chains that were hidden were destroyed.

Ever since second grade I had felt pain from the mistreatment of this teacher. When someone would mention her name, I instantly felt the hurt and pain. I didn't want to hear her name or see her face. It was that simple. And when I would hear or see her, I would get immediately angry. That went on for years.

What I didn't realize was she had been a part of my pain for all those years, and I didn't understand why. Her offenses caused me unnecessary grief that I didn't have to experience... if only I had forgiven. Just think — for thirty-six years she had impacted my life. Wow!

And at the season that I was in, God knew I didn't need to feel any worse than I was feeling. You see, my experience with her had opened a door that I couldn't shut, and this door had affected every area of my life. I had unknowingly given her the power to rule what feelings and emotions I would apply to myself and others. Jesus! I am so glad that God realized that I was not free. I had been chained for over thirty years. I was chained to her and the offenses and pain that she had caused. I had allowed this one person and her hateful offenses to imprison me for over thirty years. Knowing now what I didn't know then, how simple my freedom could have been had I just applied a simple "I forgive you" and released it.

By not forgiving her, every relationship I had was overshadowed by my pain. It instantly caused me to mistrust and build a wall for others so that they could never successfully get close to the real me. There were places in my heart that no one had access or entrance to. I was not on lockdown from the outside, but I was on lockdown from within, and left to spend a life sentence in solitary confinement until God reduced my sentence and set me free.

That is why when God mentioned her name, I began to weep like a little girl. And I asked Him, "Why am I feeling this pain over a second grade teacher? And why won't You make it stop?" God knew that in order to heal me, He had to heal the little girl trapped inside of me. I love God because that day was the day that He used my pain to set the little girl free.

I asked God why He didn't do it sooner. And God told me, "You never asked me to heal you from it, so I couldn't take it until you were ready to let it go." That day on the floor of my bedroom at the age of forty-three, I forgave my second grade teacher and was set free from the pain of her offenses. She was not there for me to physically confront, but emotionally and in my heart I had to let the anger and bitterness go. I had to charge her with the offenses. Was she guilty? Yes. Did it hurt? Yes. But the next move had to be mine. I was the only one who could let it go. She was not serving the prison sentence, I was. Her actions didn't build a prison for her, but my unforgiveness had built my prison. And it was obvious that I had been living there for quite some time. The cruel and mean things she did to me were not imprisoning her, but they had imprisoned me. God didn't need to release her. He needed to set me free.

It was me who was being emancipated in the hills of Tennessee on Booker Farm Rd., because it was not my teacher who had lost her freedom, it was me. I was the one on lockdown, and it was a proven fact that many of my life decisions and choices were affected because of my inability to forgive. It is like Mother Wright always says, "Unforgiveness is like *me* taking poison and hoping that *you* will die."

So, let me put it to you this way. If a thief steals your purse, you can forgive him, but he may never hold or have access to your purse or even you again. You can forgive him without ever seeing him again because *forgiveness starts in you.* Will you ever have a relationship with him or have an encounter with him again? I would say maybe yes, or maybe no. It all depends on how close he was to you. Was this person a stranger or someone you knew? You must also consider whether you can and will trust this person again, because trust and forgiveness are two separate things.

Another thing you must take into consideration is that life is just life, and it has a way of keeping you together or pulling you apart. I think if life positions you in a place where you can interact with each other, then when you meet again it could be possible to form a relationship with this person if both parties are willing.

The main thing is when you think of this person in your heart, you are not angry, mad, or bitter. This person simply has no more effect on you. Yes, they were wrong, but you have chosen to forgive them, and by doing so, in turn, you become free.

Let's pray:

Father, in the name of Jesus, thank You Lord for giving me the freedom of forgiveness. Thank You for freeing me from the pain and guilt of my past that I once carried. I also want to thank You for letting me know that I no longer have to bear them. Thank You for releasing me from my past and the prison I was in. I thank You for freeing the little girl who was locked up inside of me. You knew that it was the little

girl that hindered me from loving and receiving love from others, and I thank You. It is because she is free that I can freely give love. It is a great honor and a blessing to know that You understand how to heal me where I hurt, even when I don't know what I am hurting from. God, You are awesome and Your love is indescribable. You are the greatest Father that a daughter could ever hope for. Your loving and protecting hand can reach beyond present, past, and future events to make us complete. I love You for being God, Savior, Ruler, and Redeemer in my life. That is why I cry Abba, Father! Lord, You are so loving and caring — You are amazing. I am glad that You chose me to be Your child. God, I give to You all of the praise, glory, and honor. From Your daughter, these things I pray and ask in the name of Jesus Christ.

Amen

Chapter Seven
God, Please Heal the Families

*N*ow do you understand why it is important to walk in the spirit of forgiveness at all times? Because there are places in our lives that we struggle with and we carry the scars of rejection and disappointment. It is not enough to only walk in forgiveness in the house of God — we must also apply it to our jobs and in every relationship that we have. We must practice it in our communities, and especially in our homes, because what we practice in our personal lives will spill over into our spiritual relationships.

It appears that in our local assemblies we are seeing a pattern, and that pattern is we do not understand how to relate to and respect each other. We have not placed God in the center of our relationships. And so, because we won't forgive our families and friends, it has become a carry-over into our ministries. We are bringing our chaotic environments from home, work, and our communities into the church, and our relationships with our sisters and brothers in Christ are being greatly affected.

That is why we can't place a finger on why we have such a great problem with unforgiveness in the house of God. It is because our ministries are a reflection of our family environment. Guess what? The behavior of what we see in the house of God is a mirror of what we see in our families. By our natural families being so dysfunctional, so are our relationships in our church families. If we can successfully get our families healed, we can get our churches healed.

Let's look at what is really happening, and let's get our heads out of the sand for a minute. The family structure as we know it is perishing. The divorce rate is off the charts. We have more one-parent homes than ever. Our men are making babies and leaving, not to mention the sisters, who are now leaving, too. No one will make a solid commitment to each other and the children are suffering. Rather than marry, they choose to settle for common law marriages — or should I say, like my mama would say, "Let's just shack up." And this leaves an unhealthy example for the children to follow. These examples say it's okay not to stay or commit to a relationship, so now we have a generation that is afraid of commitment and finds it easy to abandon everything in their lives because they saw examples of no commitment in their parents.

So, when the pressures of life come, they take the easy way out. They refuse to stick to it, stay, and tough it out. They don't commit to education, employment, friends, family, or any other life choices.

Just think — all of this is because Mom and Dad displayed for them the perfect example of failure, which was do not commit, just leave. When it gets hard, just bail. It is easier, anyway. What a cowardly way out, people. Look at the mess we are in. Think about it — what if God quit on us?

What I want the reader to understand is I am not speaking from a perspective of what I've *heard*; I am relating to you what I've *experienced*. Both of my children's fathers were never completely committed to the relationship, so I ended up raising my children without them. Did they come out okay beneath all of the mess and drama of my past? So far, I can say yes.

It would be impossible to take any credit for the way that their lives have developed. But what I can say is I placed God in my home and no matter what the circumstances were, God became a solid foundation. So you see, it was God who made up the difference in my family for all the mistakes that I made. That is why if we can get God to become the center of our families, He has the ability to change every wrong decision you have ever made for the better. We know that all things work together for the good of those who love Him and are called according to His purpose. In my pursuit of God, I found out that God can cancel a negative with a positive. What a mighty God we serve! God can and will make the difference.

Can you now see why the house of God has a hard time getting people to commit? If they won't commit to God or themselves, how can we expect them to commit to the work of God? Do you see the weak structure of the family and the effect that it has on the body of Christ? We need healing!

Check it out. The wife refuses to submit to the husband. Why? Because of lack of trust and unforgiveness. So, now she comes to the house of God and will not submit to anyone. And the reason for this is simply because the pattern has been set in her relationship at home. Her home environment becomes her place of authority and control. We can call it her "safe place." This is the place where she rules. Because of her insecurities, she refuses to allow anyone other than herself in her space to lead. Due to her pain, she has learned only to trust in herself. Her problem is she wants to let go, but she is too afraid to let go. And it's all because the people in her past have failed her and because she can't process her pain. She feels everyone will do the same thing to her. So, she is afraid to trust.

Therefore, when her leader is trying to lead her, she finds it difficult because of her trust issues and insecurities. When she tried before there was no commitment to her care and well-being. She was forced to lead even if she didn't want to. For her it becomes difficult to follow because she has always taken the leadership role whether she wanted it or not.

And maybe the reason that she is always leading is because she has lost her ability to trust anyone but herself. So often women are placed in positions of "make it happen or let it all fall apart." When placed in these positions, guess what happens? If she is a real woman, she will take the lead before she sees her family and the people she loves fall apart. During these times she feels abandoned and betrayed. And if left in this position, her view and confidence in men becomes zero because she has been wounded and neglected. Guess what, readers? This is not hearsay; this is my life and the pain of it all. It has nothing to do with the church; it is a trust issue that she brings to the church. And because of it, the church and those in the church suffer from it. When we see relationships involving hurting people, we must learn to put things in the proper perspective. These behaviors we see are not behaviors that we were born with; these are behaviors that we have learned and adapted to because of our environment.

Another thing I would like to bring to the reader's attention is I strongly believe that the reason many of the men in the house of God find it difficult to lead is because they have never been forced to lead in their own family environment. Many have found ways to allow the women in their lives to rule and structure the family.

These men take the easy road to avoid the responsibilities of leadership. They hide under their inadequacies. When the difficult task of making decisions presents itself, they shrink back in a non-aggressive position and allow the overbearing and controlling women in their lives the opportunity to lead. Again, this is not hearsay, but my reality. Look at the disorder of our families. Do you think it will stop at home? No sir — it is spilling over in our relationships in God's house.

Women, the order of God is that the men are the leaders and we must allow them the space and the ability to lead. We have to learn to trust God until they become effective leaders. I found out when we don't step back and give them that opportunity, we are only weakening the family unit. Anything with two heads is perverted. That is why, ladies, God did not call you to lead — He called him. Ladies, God called us the "help meet." We are only there to help him meet what he cannot. We are not placed there to do it for him; we are there to support him while he does it. Look at yourself as a support beam in the relationship.

Don't weaken your man's ability by demanding that he follow your lead. Pull back a little, and become the cheerleader that God has created you to be. It won't weaken who you are, it will just strengthen his love for you. Let him lead. I am sure he would love that.

And the same thing applies to the children. They are not required to obey their parents, so they come to the house of God and no one can get them to do anything. They won't behave or obey. Many will not follow leadership and they are disruptive. And you will find that they do it because they feel that they have their parents' support. There is no discipline at home, so they refuse discipline in the house of God. The family structure is lacking discipline, compassion, and love. No one loves each other at home, and they show no respect, so they come to church and have no love or respect. Our family structure is hurting badly, and until we identify what the real problem is and seek God to repair it, the house of God will continue to be an unhealthy environment.

Consider this for a moment. If we, as believers, identify the problems in our homes and fix them, think of the healthy environment that would result in the place of worship, because real worship starts at home. What would happen if we didn't wait to get to church and worship, but we worshipped in our homes? What would happen if we taught our children how to worship at home? The reality of it all is real commitment starts at home. Real love and forgiveness start at home.

That is why we have gangs taking over our

communities. It is because our youth are looking for someone who will make a real commitment to them. What they are really saying is, "I am searching for a family that will not leave, no matter what happens." They are seeking a family unit that will be there during the good, the bad, and the ugly. The youth in these gangs are screaming, "We want commitment!" And rather than having no commitment at all, I will attach myself to people with no integrity or morals. Can't you see the importance of commitment and the danger of the lack of it?

Everything that we are or ever hope to become will begin in our family environment — our personalities, our likes, and dislikes, many of our habits, and the list goes on. It starts at home first. I can't be one thing at home and come to church and try to be who and what I am not. After a while of pretending, the real me will show up. It will never fit. I am what I am.

I worked for the General Motors automobile company for over seventeen years, and they understood the principle of family. They believed if they could keep our home environment calm, we would come to work peaceful and be more productive because we would have less stress. That is why they offered legal services, family counseling, and many other things to help fix the family climate.

We have to be careful with the choices we make because they are not only affecting the individual, but they affect everyone they are attached to. My husband would tell me that his drug habit wasn't hurting anyone but himself. How untrue that was. It was destroying the fiber of our whole family unit. Not only was he hurting himself, he was hurting me, my children, his parents, and everyone who cared about him. His choices affected us all.

Look at what Satan did in the Garden. Because of one ungodly choice that our parents Adam and Eve made, he used them to destroy the family unit. He separated us from our Father by sin, and look at the effects it caused. It destroyed the fellowship and peace of the family. It caused disharmony. The first brother Cain killed the second brother Abel. And the families of the earth have been fighting ever since.

David is another example. He had some serious issues because of a choice that was made and his whole family suffered because of it. And our family structure is suffering because of the choices we are making — and so are our ministries. They go hand in hand.

If we pay close attention to what happened with David's children and his family, we will note that it was brought on because of an ungodly desire for a relationship that God never intended for him to have. What ungodly relationships are we investing in outside of our families?

Don't get me wrong — it did not catch God off-guard because He knows all things. But that is not to say that this relationship was intended for David to partake in. David should have been disciplined enough to not have allowed himself to become a part of it. But as we study this story closer, David was out of place physically, spiritually, and emotionally.

You might say, "How can that be?" Any time

you are not doing the things that God has ordained for you to do, you fall into temptation and everything about you is out of order. *2 Samuel 11:1 — And it came to pass, after the year was expired, at the time when kings go forth to battle, that David sent Joab, and his servants with him, and all Israel; and they destroyed the children of Ammon, and besieged Rabbah. But David tarried still at Jerusalem.*

David was in a season that kings were to go to war, but he stayed home. He was physically out of place. He should have been at war. By staying home, David was doing something out of the character of kings. Any time you step out of your position in the Kingdom, you fall into the traps of the enemy.

2 Samuel 11:2 — And it came to pass in an evening tide, that David arose from off his bed, and walked upon the roof of the king's house: and from the roof he saw a woman washing herself; and the woman was very beautiful to look upon. He was on his roof and saw Bathsheba and inquired of her because she was bathing and he saw her beauty. Here we go again with that old ancient spirit of lust. The spirit of lust caused David to be spiritually out of place. Lust presented an opportunity to David, and he yielded to the temptation.

2 Samuel 11:5 — And the woman conceived, and sent and told David, and said, I am with child. ......2 Samuel 11:14-15 And it came to pass in the morning, that David wrote a letter to Joab, and sent it by the hand of Uriah. [15] And he wrote in the letter, saying,

Set ye Uriah in the forefront of the hottest battle, and retire ye from him, that he may be smitten, and die.

Then he was emotionally out of place because when Bathsheba sent word that she was with child, David no doubt became fearful of what her husband and others would think. So, he had her husband killed. He sent him to the front of the battle and commanded that Uriah was left unprotected. David was reacting out of his intellect and emotions, rather than his spiritual relationship with God. He was emotion-driven and not God-driven. Therefore, he was emotionally out of place.

This is what is going on in the body of Christ. We, as a body of people, are out of order in the Kingdom of God. We are spiritually out of place. This is a time that God is requiring that we seek healing for our families, our churches, and our communities. Yet, we continue to follow the same pattern in our every-Sunday worship services, never inquiring about the mind and the will of God. Church as usual! We are talking about battling the enemy in the house of God, but what we should be doing is teaching and empowering people on how to defeat their spiritual giants in their homes.

David was not only an ordinary man, but he was a ruler. He ruled all of Israel. And because David stepped out of the will of God, the kingdom and his family suffered. The same things are happening today because our leaders and elders are out of order. Our families and our churches are out of order and suffering. If the leaders won't stand up and teach truth, then who will teach us?

This one mistake caused David's whole

family to suffer, as well as his kingdom. Men and women of God, it only takes one unrepented mistake. It wasn't what he did that made God angry. Before David committed this act with Bathsheba, men and women throughout history had done the same thing. They had affairs or cheated with other people before this, and believe it or not, as bad as it sounds, they have killed for love. Or should I say, in David's case, for lust. But what got God angry is that David would not repent and tried to hide his sins until confronted by the prophet Nathan.

Well, guess what? The real prophets are here. They are not standing in the office of the pastor, elder or the evangelist; they are here standing in the office of the prophets challenging God's people to repent. Jeremiah and Isaiah stood before Israel and declared that everyone should repent and return back to God, because sin had ruled long enough. It was time to obey God and His laws. Can't you see the penalty of sin? It will affect everything in our lives.

Think about it. How many ungodly desires have you had? These desires have disrupted everything in your life and have caused you and your family great grief. And every one of these desires has hindered your relationship with God and affected your families, ministries, and relationships.

What mistakes are we making in our families that are causing generations to be affected? When we look at David's life, it was a time that he should have had peace, but because of his lack of discipline and restraint, what should have brought peace brought the sword to his house. And Amnon and Tamar are perfect examples of who was affected. His children were the greatest victims.

I bet you thought I had forgotten about Tamar and Amnon, but I haven't. Tamar and Amnon are the representation of the result of a father's poor judgment and the consequence of his passionate decision gone bad. And because of it, his family was left with serious problems. If we view the church family and our own personal families in comparison, we are seeing families and our churches struggling with real serious issues. These are issues we have to confront and seek God for answers. But the first place that we need to start is a place of forgiveness.

We need to ask our families to forgive us for not becoming the Godly role models that we should have become. Then we need to ask our communities to forgive us. We have neglected them by not displaying a real interest in the issues that our communities have faced culturally, economically, and spiritually. And lastly, we need to ask our ministries to forgive us because we have not committed to the pursuit of the gospel and have lost focus of the mandate of Christ. We have compromised God's Word and His laws.

Let's pray:

Father, in the name of Jesus we are in serious trouble. We need You now to heal our families, our communities, and our churches, and bring them back to You. Lord, we are losing generations because of our selfish passions. Lord, please redirect our hearts and our minds. Show us how to reach our families and teach us to lead them to the house of God. But most of all, show us how to teach them to worship in our homes. Instruct us on how to reveal to our sons and daughters a passionate desire to become children of Yours. Give them a passion so that they can teach other generations to love You also. Give us a commitment to our families and loved ones. Show us how to impact our communities and our work environment, and any area of our lives.

Lord, this world is so out of order that we don't even know where to begin to ask for Your help. But God, You are God and that is why we turn to You. Only You know what it will take to turn this world around. Please Lord, help us now because we desperately need You. We are in trouble and we need You. These things we ask in the name of Jesus Christ.

Amen

Chapter Eight
Save Our Children

I would like to bring our attention back to Tamar, Amnon, and Absalom. The bible reveals that their family structure, because of David's sin, was morally weak, full of lust, jealousy, and unforgiveness with no respect for boundaries and hatred. For generations his children suffered because of their father's choices, and today our world and families suffer with some of the same things that were in David's household.

Can you see these behaviors in our world as we know it? The way we treat each other is because we lack respect for one another. And because of the lack of respect, we suffer in our relationships and the way we interact with each other. And because we are a disrespectful generation, it seems that we have no problem disregarding one another's feelings. Even if it causes our relationships to suffer, we still insist on crossing the boundaries of disrespect. Disrespect pulls us apart, but respect places value on our relationships in its proper prospective. I want to say to everyone reading this book that respect must be one of the major elements that should fasten us together. I am just giving you food for thought.

But let's pull our attention back to David and his children, because I would like to extract one of the things that ensnared David and began his spiral downhill. I dealt with it in a previous chapter, where we identified lust as one of the driving factors of the decay of our relationships. This ungodly desire has brought kings and queens to their knees. It has destroyed empires. And when you add unforgiveness to lust, these two spirits are a very destructive force. If we take close notice of their influence, each of these spirits has the capacity and the ability to cause you to become imprisoned in every area of your life. That is why I strongly believe that these two ungodly desires were the principle motivation for what happened to Tamar by her brother Amnon. His ungodly lust provoked his plans to rape his sister Tamar, leaving her scarred and broken. We see that the horrendous violation of rape, which was motivated by lust from Amnon upon Tamar, was destructive. And these same spirits are wreaking havoc in the world as we know it. If we look closely at history, lust and unforgiveness have been in operation since the fall of humanity and they have brought with them chaos.

I would like to pose a question to you. What brought the sword to the house of David? It was lust and his desire to cover his sins. What brought sin into the world? It was the lust of the flesh, the lust of the eye, and the pride of life. Eve saw the tree of good and evil and it was pleasant to the eye (the lust of the eye). After speaking to the serpent, she was told that it would make them like God (lust of the flesh). Once they had eaten and their eyes became open, they hid — rather than repent and seek for God, they hid from Him (pride of life). When you hide a thing that is wrong it is because of pride. Your flesh doesn't want to humble itself and say, "I am not perfect and I make mistakes." And that is because flesh wants to rule over God. It wants to be like God and be perfect. But because of sin and our sinful nature, we know that could never be the case.

When we search out what happened with Adam and Eve, we immediately see that they began to cover themselves after they sinned. And the same thing happened in David's case. The moment he felt that his affair with Bathsheba would be discovered, he plotted a scheme to cover the evidence.

When we sin and we run for cover, it makes matters worse. When sin is covered, it brings bondage, but when it is exposed it brings freedom. That is why God is permitting me to pen this manuscript, so that we can uncover the dangers of these two spirits.

We must identify and completely expose these two evils that are causing many of the problems in our society, our ministries, and our world. Then the healing process will begin, once identified and exposed. I believe we will diligently seek solutions to overcome our ill fate and stand against these two forces of darkness. And I also realize that what I am doing in this writing is only scratching the surface, and there will be many more writings by me and other authors to expose these evils.

Even though we can only identify a portion of the problem, it does not benefit us if we do not search out the solution to alleviate our dilemma. It is fruitless to identify the quandary and not come up with answers to benefit the reader. The most important thing that we must discover is what will set us free.

The answer is so simple, but so overlooked. I guess because we are complex creatures and we have a vast creative ability, we find ourselves overlooking the simplicity. We love to see things from a vast, extensive, Technicolor perception or view. The more complicated it appears, the more fascinated we become. But this answer is not deep and it doesn't require a lot of research. Even though the answer is actually straightforward, we must stop and wrap our minds around its simplicity. To know that the answer will come with challenges, and what the challenges are, requires inner strength and humility.

If you really would like to know the answer, it is found in the forgiveness that God gives to us. And that forgiveness is called grace. Look at how powerful forgiveness can be. Forgiveness released all of humanity from the grips of sin.

Even though we were God's enemies, can't you see the power that forgiveness brings with it? We were an enemy of God. He could not even look at us because He was too Holy of a God to look at sin. But the Creator and Ruler of the universe worked His way through all of the obstacles of sin to buy us back from our enemy, which was Satan, our flesh, and the world system. He did not leave us like we were. But before man was created, God had a backup plan for the ones who would offend Him and become His enemies. He had a lamb already slain before the foundation of the world was formed.

Not only did God forgive us, His enemies, but He rescued, redeemed, and restored us. Please take a close look at the power of forgiveness. As I just stated, there was a lamb slain before the foundation of the world was formed. God has given to us an escape route and it was that He rescued His enemies on the cross of Calvary. Can't you see the impact of forgiveness?

And what God did for us is called the grace of God, His unmerited favor. We can't earn it, we can't buy it, we can't even fight for it. The only thing that we must do is receive and accept it.

The only requirement that God has for us to receive this gift of forgiveness is to repent. If you don't understand this concept, let me explain it to you as simply as I can. Repentance is accepting the fact that I was wrong, declaring that I will never do it again, and meaning it. It is just that simple. There is nothing deep or mysterious about it.

To be forgiven by God, we don't have to pay anything for it. God gave us this gift for free. And the only thing required from humanity is that we accept the gift. Look at how simple that is. *John 3:16 — For God so loved the world, that he gave his only begotten Son, that whosoever believeth in him should not perish, but have everlasting life.* And His son is Jesus Christ. He is the gift to all of humanity. If we accept Him and then learn to apply that same grace to others, then we will see our world, our families, our communities, and our churches healed and delivered. By God giving to us His son, He was saying to us "I forgive you for your offense of disobedience."

Look at the power of forgiveness. **God Dropped the Charges** and we were able to go free. Just as God has freely given us forgiveness, we must consciously and diligently seek to give it to our enemies and those who have offended us. Forgiveness and repentance have been proven and stand sure. But out of the entire arsenal of weapons that God has given to us, these two weapons are the ones that we greatly neglect to use. And believe it or not, these weapons should be used every day that we live. We can't use them enough and it is impossible to exhaust their power.

Not only should we apply grace and forgiveness to others, but we must learn to freely apply them to our own lives. If we would consciously learn to practice this in our families, in our communities, and within all of our relationships, then our world would change. We cannot become like David and cover our sins; we must run to God to heal and forgive us because other generations are depending on us to leave them a healthy pattern of Godliness to live by.

When we probe deeper into Tamar and Amnon's relationship, we find that it depicts incest, rape, and rejection. This may or may not be a good example to compare our family structure to, but it explores real topics worthy of discussion. And one of the topics that no one really wants to take aggressive action with is the abuse of our children.

More children in our day have been beaten, murdered, raped, and molested than ever before. And the sad part about it is they can't even escape in their own homes. A place that should be safe for them has become their war zone and a cesspool of pain. Innocent babies are experiencing things that they should not be knowledgeable of at their young and tender ages. They are forced to perform sexual acts that they should never have heard of, not to mention experience.

Look at the madness of the world that we are living in. These babies are being prostituted, forced against their little wills to perform sexual acts that they didn't even know existed. And oftentimes because of their innocence they cannot understand the perversion that it contains. The distressing part about it is the majority of them are being made to become sexual play toys right in their little homes. Many of their bedrooms have become their prisons and the environment for their violation. What should be a place of rest for them has become their torture chamber. And when the torment is over, they are instructed not to tell, and it is called the "silent secret."

So, before they have an opportunity to slightly envision their dreams of who or what they are to become, they are left with the scars of physical, mental, emotional, and sexual ex-ploitation of what some perverted adult has left their little minds to remember. They cannot see or feel intimacy without recalling a picture of the pain and abuse of their offender and the acts that they performed.

My God. What is going on in our world and what are we thinking about, people? Many of our children are forced to see their abusers occasionally, and some of them see them on a continual basis. They are their uncles, cousins, brothers, sisters, neighbors, mothers and fathers, teachers, preachers, and strangers. Is there any place safe for our babies? Heaven is crying because of the abuse of God's innocent children. The angels are weeping, and so should we.

These children have been scarred early, and are too young to understand how to forgive and be set free. They walk around in a prison cell of insecurity, anger, hatred, and bitterness. They live their lives feeling like they can never measure up to the standard of others, constantly dealing with inferiority complexes all because of their abuse. And the heartbreaking reality is they really don't understand how they got into the madness they are in. Their little innocent minds have been chained in a mental juvenile detention center. Can you imagine being in an institution and you don't even know what you have been charged with? But this one thing we do know; if they don't receive the appropriate help they need as children, these children will slide through the cracks of our society and continue the moral decay of our world.

In order to heal and build quality characteristics in these children, they need the help of trained counselors who will allow them to make sense of the abuse and the madness of their world, along with helping them process their pain. And if they do not receive the help that is needed as children, they grow up and are transferred into the adult prison facility of the mind. As adults, they are mentally and emotionally locked in a mental penal system, and, to be quite honest, they are the victims. Rather than a short-term sentence, they are facing life imprisonment. They are charged with guilt, anger, frustration, rebellion, insecurity, inferiority, and low self-esteem, all because of an abuser. These adults struggle most of their whole lives with their hidden pain and the lack of ability to process the offense that they received as a child.

They walk around the majority of their lives with a ball and chain on. And that ball and chain is called *offense*. The pain and abuse that they are chained to inhibits them from the freedom to live full and productive lives. That is why you see many of them self-destruct early with addiction, and even grow up and become the abusers.

I prophetically speak that the anger of the Lord is kindled greatly against us. And when I say "us" I mean all of us, because we have not fought with a vengeance to put a stop to this madness. God is holding us accountable for our part in closing our eyes and not waging war against these evil spirits of perversion and lust that are killing our babies.

Satan is a master at war. He has studied his opponent. He understands that if he strikes early during childhood development, his chances of crippling these children for life are almost foolproof. You know the game that he plays and the rules of this deadly game. He attacks and sends abuse and offenses before you are old enough to understand how to process the pain. I call it hitting below the belt. Our families are hurting, and so are our communities and churches — all because we were hurt by someone and we could not get over the pain.

That is why in the house of God, or even in our families and communities, we cannot be afraid to confront the undesirable issues — because our families are depending on us! We must confront them and address them with a passion. We cannot afford to continue to see the big pink elephant in the room and walk around it as if it is not there. Yet we are constantly feeding it, and it is increasingly growing.

Our dark secrets have to be exposed so that we, as the body of Christ, can be healed. Yes, it is going on in our churches. There are little children sitting in our congregations who have been physically, mentally, and emotionally abused and we look the other way. Until we stand up and do something about it, both our nation and our world will continue to decline and decay.

The bible tells us that judgment must first begin in the house of God. And after we have dealt with these issues, only then will it give us the ability to apply healing to others inside and outside of God's house. We have to face these ungodly issues head on.

Let's say a prayer:

Father, in the name of Jesus we are crying out to You for our innocent babies. Lord, please send Your angels to protect every child that is walking on this earth. Protect them from the evil that is surrounding them. Give them shelter and food to eat. And supply the love that they need. Give them all the love and comfort that they require. Help them to feel a sense of security. Those who are being abused, and the abuse, are hidden. Expose their abusers and move those

children out of danger.

Give us the funds and the facilities to meet the needs of the innocent victims. Place these babies with loving parents who will care for them and show them the love and kindness that they desire to have. Allow these babies an opportunity to enjoy their childhood without pain. I know, Lord, that it is a great thing, but with You, Lord, nothing is too large and no matter is too small.

We need You to stir our hearts and our minds so that we will make laws that will give more protection to our children. Expose the teachers, preachers, mothers, fathers, sisters, brothers, friends, and strangers that are wounding our little babies. Hold them accountable for all of their evil deeds and actions.

We need Your strength and help. Please God, hear our cries and cover our babies. In the name of Jesus Christ...

Amen

Chapter Nine
Will the Real Leaders Please Stand Up!

*W*hen we, as believers, refuse to face and address the painful problems we are wrestling with and neglect to get to the core of the real dilemma, it allows our sinful nature the ability to cover them with dark lies and deception. It is when these corrupt seeds of ungodliness become hidden and unspoken that they take root and grow, and become a part of our makeup. And we struggle sometimes for years to be set free. Isn't it sad that we find ways to cover the truth and settle for the lies? And the reason that we do this is because of our sinful, fleshly, and carnal nature. Without the leading of God's spirit we are always driven to darkness, and that darkness is sin.

So, you see, that is why I can't over look the story of Tamar and Amnon. When confronted with his ungodly passion, Amnon and Jonadab went straight to the dark side. In this story, Amnon was suffering from depression because of his lustful desires. And rather than Jonadab telling Amnon the truth and confronting his perverted emotions, he helped to place the nails in Tamar's coffin.

What a sad story. Look at the pain that she could have been spared. If only Jonadab, the person Amnon took counsel from, would have spoken up with integrity. He should have said, "Look, man, you are sick. You can't do that to your sister — it's crazy." At that point Jonadab had an opportunity to become a man of integrity and wisdom, and he would have been known in the pages of this book as a person who had given good and sound counsel and diverted a tragic event.

This is a clear illustration of what I am speaking of. It could have been a perfect example to see the benefits of a real leader taking a stand. But rather than stand for what was right, he sided with evil — the reason being Jonadab was as tainted as Amnon. And because of his ungodly position, he fueled the fire for the sexual abuse of Tamar.

Jonadab did not stand for what was right. That is why I am making a comparison of these two friends, their association with each other, and their deviant thinking. There is a saying that says great minds think alike, but I will also say that sick minds do, too.

In our family structure and our relationships we have to shift our thinking and hold each other responsible, because, my sisters and brothers, if we want change we have to change our passive approach and deal with the tough subjects — things like the one in the last chapter on child abuse, and so many other concerns that our world is facing. We have the neglect of the elderly, medical reform, poverty levels, unfair job markets, and so many other things that are dividing our world. You know — the ones no one wants to talk about, and if they do talk about it, they never apply any action to resolve them. Men and women, we have to get a grip on these problems. And we must do it quickly if we expect other generations to survive and have a healthy view of life.

When a situation presents itself, we need

good leaders to step up to the plate and make sound judgments. In this story, because a man who was willing to succumb to the sick passion of a friend, an innocent young lady was crushed. Jonadab did not use sound judgment. There was a chance for Amnon's friend to make sense of something that was crazy, and he didn't. When Amnon told his friend Jonadab of his desire for Tamar, rather than Jonadab reasoning with Amnon concerning his unhealthy desire for his sister, his friend fed his lustful thinking. Jonadab plotted out a well-put-together scheme that allowed Amnon to rape his sister.

Look at the mind of the person that Amnon was associated with. He placed his confidence in someone who would help him devise an evil plan to rape his own sister. How sick is that? When lust is the main ingredient, you will find satisfaction with anyone who will help you satisfy that lustful desire. Amnon found comfort in Jonadab's plan because his passion outweighed his reasoning. Amnon's actions and cravings were perverted and sick, and the scheme of his friend Jonadab was even more distorted.

Amnon was receiving advice from a spiritually and morally weak individual, and it was fleshly counsel. The bible says in *Psalm 1:1* — *How blessed is the man who does not walk in the counsel of the wicked, nor stand in the path of sinners, nor sit in the seat of scoffers!*

People, we need to watch who we walk, stand, and sit with. We cannot afford to receive unhealthy counsel just because we want to satisfy the lust of our flesh. We cannot accept the guidance of these leaders as the body of Christ. And not only as the body of Christ, but as people in general. Stop allowing wolves in sheep's clothing to speak to you or over you. Their motives are corrupt and cunning, and they are very subtle in their approach. The bible tells us to watch, as well as pray. We must learn to passionately try every spirit to see if they are of God.

You have to stop listening to men and women who have studied your weaknesses and have recognized how to monopolize upon your inefficiencies so that they can satisfy their sinful, greedy, and unhealthy agendas. They are predators waiting for an opportunity to take full advantage of your broken and painful situation to manipulate it for their benefit.

Just as there are snakes and vipers waiting to take advantage of you in the world, so are there snakes and vipers waiting on you in the local fellowship. We must open our eyes and stop being naïve, believing that everybody in the house of God is there because they love God. Some people are there because they come to see who will become their next victim.

Remember, Jesus said there will be false prophets and they will come in sheep's clothing. Open your eyes and see the realness of it all. Not everybody dancing and shouting and speaking in tongues beside you in the sanctuary is in love with you or God. But what they do love is what God has to offer. They want to enjoy the benefits of God, but not live a life that will please God. These individuals want just enough of God to be dangerous. They know how to manipulate and deceive innocent men and women who are sincerely in love with God. That is why they are watching, to see if you are the weakest link.

I do not want to leave you feeling as if every leader is out for no good, because that would be untrue. But what you need to know is, just as there are bad leaders, there are also genuine, good leaders who will lead you in the right direction.

That is why I am saying, will the real leaders please, please stand up! We need to see you and be able to identify you. We are pleading for you to please stop hiding and take center stage! I am begging you to reveal yourselves! The world is seeking leaders that have no hidden agendas, and just want to be known as men and women of integrity and compassion. We are searching for the men and women who will not compromise the moral fiber of God or our society. They will stand for truth. I say again: Will the real leaders please stand up! For God's sake, we really need you. And we are crying out for you to come out of hiding and make a difference.

What has happened today is we see so many phony leaders. We have settled for their charismatic presentation and views of life and the gospel. We have become fascinated by their gifts and not their Godly lifestyles. We are following their soothing words, but those words have no power to heal or deliver. We have learned to use artificial sweeteners rather than real, pure sugar. Yes, we have settled for margarine rather than butter, because margarine costs less. These are the people who have not made the true conversion into holiness. They are not willing to make the sacrifice to do what it takes to be anointed.

To be anointed you have to pay a great price, but to be charismatic costs little. You can find it on every shelf and in every corner. You can find these leaders in storefront churches, and whether you want to believe it or not, they are even in the mega ministries. It is like cancer — it is spreading everywhere.

Many have mass-produced concepts and messages that carry with them no weight of the anointing and no power to deliver. These false leaders hold the ability to captivate listeners with their manipulation and their persuasion, and cause them to surrender to their fleshly schemes. And the reason these ruthless leaders are able to entice the masses is because we are a "right now" "hurry up" generation and we don't want to wait on God. So, we settle for the cheap substitutes. But what we don't realize is, if it is going to be a real change, it will take the anointing of God to do it. It is the anointing that destroys the yoke! If we are going to be set free, it has to be by the power of God.

Men and women, we must seek out good, honest, and Godly leaders. And when we find them, we must submit and allow them the opportunity to pour into our lives. We must look for men and women of God who display a life of Godliness, and we must stand still long enough for them to speak into our lives.

We have to allow these leaders who are showing integrity and have a clear understanding of God's Word to train and mentor us. As God's children, we must give support to these leaders who are displaying for us a true lifestyle of righteousness and holiness. It is a mandate that we seek them out and hold up their arms prayerfully, mentally, emotionally, and financially, so that they do not grow weary in their assignment in the Kingdom of God. These are the leaders we should humbly seek to submit ourselves to so they can effectively lead and instruct us in the Word of God so we can gain victory over the kingdom of darkness. We should respect the sacrifices they have made to learn and know the principles of God by having an ear to receive the directions of God for this generation, leaving a clear map for other generations to follow. We have got to submit and follow the guidance of these men and women of integrity, and allow these leaders to discipline and instruct us as children of God. These leaders are equipped with the answers that will reveal to us the mind and the will of God for our lives. We must submit and become obedient to their leadership so that, without confrontation, they can speak into our lives. We should have a great degree of respect for these men and women of God because they are willing to be held accountable to a body of seasoned elders who will hold them accountable to live a life of Godliness so that they won't misguide God's people.

I feel that our major problem is the people we covenant with and consent to lead the body of Christ and our world reveal to us a reflection of what Jonadab presented to Amnon. They agree with our lustful and ungodly passions. Look clearly at the comparison in the scriptures in II Samuel, Chapter 13. Amnon took counsel from a friend (Jonadab) who didn't bring him any sound reasoning or conviction because Jonadab was subtle and cunning.

We have leaders who are running our churches and our government who, in order to satisfy one another's corrupt desires, are willing to sell out innocent people. Jonadab was as selfish as Amnon, and so was the counsel that he provided.

This thing was so sin-sick that they were willing to break the laws of God. And we have the same things going on in our world — no one will respect the laws of God. We refuse to honor God and His commandments. It seems as if America has taken God out of everything that concerns our nation. The essence of our country is weak and sickly. We have allowed prayer and God to be taken out of the schools, so the children have replaced Him with guns and knives and gangs. We removed God from our government and we replaced Him with a moral decay of greed, poverty, prejudice, hatred — and don't forget inequality.

Any time you leave God out of anything, you open the door for every evil thing imaginable to enter and take full occupancy. God's commandments give us a clear concept of what is right and what is wrong.

When we clearly look at these two friends, they were not only willing to break the laws of God, they were willing to conspire to destroy the life of an innocent virgin and she became the victim of their cruel conspiracy. It is the bible that plainly has instructions concerning this action: *Leviticus 18:9 — The nakedness of thy sister, the daughter of thy father, or daughter of thy mother, whether she be born at home, or born*

abroad, even their nakedness thou shalt not uncover. But because of his lust for his sister, Amnon was willing to forsake the laws of God, and so was Jonadab. His friend was a blind guide and corrupt counsel. Jonadab's heart was as dark as Amnon's. Isn't it sad that he was led by a man who had not even considered or challenged the immoral implication of Amnon's actions?

Jonadab gave him a plan on how to carry out his incestuous infatuation for his sister. He told him to make himself appear sick, and "when your father comes to see you, tell him to allow Tamar to prepare some food for you." What a sick and perverted scheme to do to someone you said you loved. Amnon had one thing in mind, and that was to satisfy his lustful appetite. Isn't it a twisted plot?

It only takes one opportunity to stand up for righteousness. But when you surround yourself with people who think and act like you, you have no one to challenge your indiscretions. If you encompass yourself with bitter, hateful, and unforgiving people, who will reveal to you your flaws? Where is the balance? And who will help you see yourself? These kinds of people are hurting, and so are you.

Look at the wicked counsel that Amnon received from Jonadab on how to have his way with Tamar. If he had shared his desire with someone of wisdom, the outcome might have been totally different. But it was obvious that they both had the same evil perception of what was the right thing to do.

Church, where are we and when will we please stand up, because the truth of the matter is if we have the same weak counsel in the house of God, we are in big trouble. We have inadequate leaders keeping each other's dark secrets and covering each other's sins so that they won't destroy their reputations. Okay, I said it, and I am not taking it back. And the sad part about it is these false leaders cast a shadow on perfectly wonderful leaders because the world can't separate the good from the bad. They are grouped together.

Let's say a prayer:

Father, in the name of Jesus, we desperately come to You because we are in trouble. Our world is falling apart and our leaders are refusing to lead us with truth and integrity. They are compromising Your truths and are settling for the least confrontational approach. God, raise up men and women who will not shrink in fear and intimidation of what is not righteous, but will hold on to what is right in Your eyes. Give them the strength of Heaven to lead the nations and heal our world, and give them discernment to know the difference between good and evil, fighting for what is right and resisting what is wrong. Lord, we need some Moseses and Joshuas of our day who will lead us to victory. Father, it is our humble desire that You please strengthen our apostles, prophets, evangelists, pastors, elders, teachers, and all of those who labor in the gospel so that they can give to us sound instructions. Lord, we need You to give us good, Godly, governmental

leaders to lead our world. And Lord, give them a heart to only obey You. We come boldly to You because You are the only one who can fix and heal us. Thank You, Lord, because I am assured that You will answer and deliver. These things we ask in Your son's name, in the name of Jesus Christ...

Amen

Chapter Ten
Stop the Cover-up!

*W*hen you look closely at what is going on in the church among our leaders, it is like there is a code of silence. When I became a believer, I was told not to let the world see what was going on in the church — especially if it had to do with something that was wrong or would cause the world to see some of our indiscretions. They told me it was called "church business." If it is bad, keep your mouth shut. They said don't air our dirty laundry. The reason I believe they said this was because it appeared that they wanted to present a perfect image in the house of God to the unbeliever...even though we know that this image is far from true.

If we really take a close look at the damage we are producing by presenting this image, we will see that it is not only destroying the body of Christ, but it has become a hindrance to the unbeliever. The picture that we don't want the sinner to see is that we are not perfect. And by not allowing them to see our imperfections, this approach alone is choking the effectiveness out of our ability to reach them.

The world is using our so-called perfection in the house of God to condemn the body of Christ. And rightfully so, if you say that you are perfect and I see improprieties. However, any sound and rational individual would draw the conclusion that you are not what you say you are.

We have presented to the world a place that appears (from the outside) to be a perfect, loving place to come to — one without blemish. And anyone who has been in the body of Christ for any length of time knows that this is just not so. What we understand as believers about the body of Christ is we have the good, the bad, and the ugly. But what keeps us hanging in for the long haul is we have a phenomenal God that makes sense of it all. And this is what the world needs to know.

We are living in an imperfect world, and we are an imperfect people in love with a perfect God. And He is the one who makes sense of what is slightly imperfect. He is the foundation that covers all of our scars, blemishes, and dark spots.

We have not successfully displayed to the unbeliever that we are desperately in great need of God's grace as believers. They have to know that at various instances we need the grace of God applied to each and every one of our lives. God's mercy is something that is necessary for us on a continual basis. We have neglected to reveal that we are only human, and we do fail, and it is only the grace of God that restores and delivers us.

The body of Christ is painting for the unbeliever an image of perfection that the unbeliever feels they cannot obtain. And the truth of the matter is, neither can we. Without the grace and mercy of God applied to us, we are left without hope. That is why it seemed to me that we had a secret code of ethics, and this code allowed us to keep our sin issues a secret. ***Proverbs 28:13 — He that covereth his sins shall not prosper: but whoso confesseth and forsaketh them shall***

have mercy. I explained to you in a previous chapter the danger of a cover-up and the effect that it has. Any time you cover a wrongdoing or sin you are allowing the enemy to taunt you with the cover-up. It binds you with guilt, frustration, and condemnation, leaving you feeling worse because of the transgression. If you are ever going to gain victory over your sinful makeup, there has to be a point when you decide to forsake all ungodliness and cling to righteousness. That is why, not only must you expose the sin, but you have got to forsake it.

There has to be a place inside of you that has a hunger and a desire to please God — a desire that will push you to turn away from the thing that displeases Him. It is not enough to reveal the sin; there has to be a forsaking of the sinful nature and the ungodly lifestyle. When God sees your brokenness, and that you are longing for change, He will then give you everything you need to secure the transformation within you. He will not leave you to struggle alone to become whole and complete in Him. Any time you are willing to forsake your life of sin, an alarm is sounded in Heaven that says to God and a host of angels that you are striving to be more like Him. And when God sees you yearning to be like Him, then all of Heaven joins the fight to make you be what you are aspiring to become.

The enemy knows that as long as we continue to hide and cover our sins, it keeps us stagnant and unproductive. That is why it is Satan's greatest desire that we, as a body of true believers, constantly look the other way, hide our sin, and not expose our weaknesses. He knows as long as we cover our sins, it will prevent the house of God from becoming fruitful and multiplying. And if that is the case, then whatever lacks growth and productivity will eventually dry up and die. So you see, a simple cover-up will cause you and the church, your family, your community, and government to become lifeless. If God says you will not prosper, that is what He means — even if it is in His own house.

It is Satan's wish that God's children walk around with guilt and condemnation tied around our necks because it gives him more ability to work his evil plots and schemes. Any time we cover sin, it places the enemy in the driver's seat. Could it possibly be that the image of perfection we are using as a defense to cover our flaws, and to present to a world of hurting people a representation of a perfect environment, is the very thing causing all of the damage and standing in the way of them accepting God?

Let me tell you about an experience that happened to me. During the time when I divorced my husband, I was battling things in my life that were causing great frustration. There were some financial issues we had not yet resolved and they were lingering still after the divorce. I was angry, bitter, frustrated, and very hurt at the time.

Well, one day while I was talking to my husband about the debt, hoping to get a resolution, we had a very disturbing falling-out. I want to stop here and pray that you, the reader, will take time and see this from my position of brokenness. And what I need you to understand is this was a very painful season of my life. A marriage that should

155

have lasted a lifetime had come to an end, and I was totally exhausted from the pain and the drama of the marriage and the divorce. If you have never experienced a divorce and betrayal, you may never understand the full impact of this kind of pain. It is like a death or the loss of someone you love. But the only difference between a divorce and death is you realize that you can see the person again and relive the pain. Death is final, but divorce never ends as long as the two of you live.

Hurting people hurt other people. And during this time we were both hurting. So, my husband would be very sarcastic. I am sure it was because of some things that I had done to wound him. What I want to admit is that my marriage did not end only because of him. I want to take my share of the blame in the marriage dissolving. I believe that is why he said things that greatly provoked me concerning the matter. Regardless of the circumstances, I was at the breaking point and I had taken all that I could take. I was like Popeye. "I done stood all I can stands and I can't stands no more!"

Many of you will try to judge me, and that's okay, because that was one of the seasons in my life where I truly saw the grace of God and His power to restore. That is why you cannot afford to judge me because some of you are just a prayer away from a meltdown yourselves. And it is only the grace of God that is keeping you right now. Let's not play games. Let's just keep it real. It is only by God's grace and mercy that we are not experiencing an everyday meltdown.

Now, back to what I was saying. On that

day, my fellow friends in the gospel, I want to tell you I was pushed right over the edge. As I remember, I was not pushed — I was shoved! And believe you me, when I tell you I fell (and boy, did I fall hard), I lost all sense of reality because I had reached my breaking point and I was at the point of no return. There was a song that we used to sing that said "Don't push me 'cause I'm close to the edge. I'm trying not to lose my head. Sometimes I wonder how I keep from going under." Well, my sisters and brothers, when I started sliding, I slid completely under and when I finally stopped, ouch! It hurt!

Before I knew it, the old girl had surfaced and every ungodly word I had forgotten...guess what? I was reintroduced to them as if they had never left (if you know what I mean). All of a sudden for that brief moment these four-letter words came out like rapid fire. They were spilling from my mouth like a machine gun that was wide open. You would have thought I was in the Vietnam War the way these words were coming out. I used some four-letter words I had forgotten even existed.

After having the meltdown, I immediately became very guilty, which I should have been because there was no God in my behavior at all. I began to weep and grieve because of the things I had said. Boy, I literally cried for days. I realized that I had misrepresented God and I knew that the enemy was going to use it against me. I was very hurt because I had allowed myself to be pushed to a place that was totally ungodly.

The Lord spoke to me and said, "Joyce, you

did it and I know that you are sorry for doing it."
God said, "If you remain silent and allow the Devil
to tell the story for you, he can paint the picture the
way that he chooses; but if you repent and confess
it openly, you have the ability to take the pen out of
his hand. He then has nothing to tell because you
have told it all yourself."

So, guess what I did? I told on myself. I took
the Devil's power and he had nothing to condemn
me with. God had forgiven me, and by me getting it
out in the open, I could begin to forgive myself.

By confessing your sins, you strip the enemy
of his ability to torment you with guilt and
frustration. You strip him of his wicked power of
condemnation. So, when someone asked me about
the incident I could, without a guilty conscience,
say, "Yes I did it and I have been forgiven for it."
That was the day I learned a valuable lesson. I
learned how to take the enemy's power.

Remember that the Devil is a liar, and that
is what he wants us to become. His desire is that
we cover our sins and walk around as hypocrites
and liars, carrying with us the shadow of guilt and
condemnation. The Devil realizes that if he can
keep us with little dark secrets, he can continue to
condemn us. The bible tells us in *1 John 1:9 — If
we confess our sins, he is faithful and just to
forgive us our sins, and to cleanse us from all
unrighteousness.* In order to be a clean church,
we have to confess. It is time to stop hiding,
because if we are going to settle for our dark secrets
in the house of God, then we are no better than the
rest of the world.

When I gave my life to God, I didn't come to

the church to receive from the body of Christ the same answers that the world would give me. I could have stayed in the world and gotten that. You might not want to believe it, but there are some pretty wise people in the world and they have some great answers. But what they don't have is the heart and the mind of God. And that is what gives the believer the cutting edge. The edge that I am speaking about is God. Because whether you believe it or not, God is the main ingredient that makes the difference in our lives and causes our image to mirror Him. And that being the case, we must offer everyone seeking for Him a clear picture of His image.

That is why when I came to a place where people said that they knew Him, I expected to see an environment that looked like Him. I was tired of what I had, and that is why I came seeking a different way of life. But when I got to His house, I did not receive exactly what I had expected to receive. The lesson I learned was the only way I could receive it was through Him.

And in order to receive that way of life, I had to be willing to take my worldly garments off and put on the robe of righteousness, and that robe is only found in Christ Jesus. There has to be a separating line. People of God, we don't need a cover-up. We need men and women of God to man up and have Godly integrity and live Godly lives.

Let's get it out there and let's deal with it so we can get healed. We have leaders who gather together board members who will support their ungodly and unfruitful plans. They are selecting people as elders and leaders, and positioning them

on governing boards that will agree with their
every decision. These men and women are placed in
spiritual rankings that they are not anointed for or
even equipped to handle in God. Their weaknesses
in God hinder them from challenging or seeking
God for truth and repentance. And while they are
in these positions of authority, they are left with no
strength or integrity and very little accountability.
Therefore, when they are faced with issues of
indiscretion they cannot humbly and compassion-
ately challenge any poor judgment concerning their
leaders' character or their sinful lifestyle. And
because of the lack of quality leadership and
guidance in the body of Christ, we see powerful and
mighty leaders continue in sin and fall victim to the
plot and plans of Satan. The sad thing about it is
they are chosen by God to do the work of God, but
they have never been challenged concerning their
Godly — or should I say *ungodly* — dispositions.
Because no one will be brave enough to question
their decisions or their sinful nature, the body of
Christ falls victim to their carelessness, which
leaves us living in a time like they lived in during
the book of Judges. Every man did what was right
in his own eyes.

When we see Jonadab in these scriptures as
the only one who saw Amnon's behavior and
recognized his grief, it lets us know that he had an
opportunity to intervene. But rather than take a
stand for right, he gave instructions on how to
satisfy Amnon's lustful appetite. This is when the
cover-up should have been exposed.

Church, because we are not getting things
out in the open, as I have said throughout the

pages of this book, we are battling the spirits of lust and unforgiveness and these enemies are destroying our families, our communities, our government, and our churches. We have to confront and expose these evils, but it must be done with Godly wisdom.

Can't you see the dangers of these two evils? Lust and unforgiveness will cause you to select people who will support your cause even if the cause is corrupt and spiteful to others. It is just a cover-up to hide the real issues. It causes you to seek counsel from only those who will help you satisfy your desires, and you will connect with people who will agree with your twisted schemes.

In the Word of God you will find examples for every behavior that humanity will ever face. That is why the story of Tamar has within it so many things that we can relate to in our world today and all of its brokenness.

By reading the story of Tamar and Amnon, it allowed me to look closely at the association of the people that I had chosen to be a part of my life. My sinful life had caused me to partner with individuals who supplied me with no balance or stability. They were incapable of pulling out of me the best that was in me.

I understand now that I chose these individuals because they helped to feed my insecurities. They were the friends who did not have the ability to challenge any of my weak areas of indiscretion because they were weak and struggling themselves. When I stare at the big picture, I see I was surrounded by people just like me — wounded, bleeding, and hurting. No, I didn't engage in the consumption of the substance on the same level that they did, but I was just as dysfunctional as they were.

That is why I stayed connected for seventeen years to a man who was hurting, broken, and wounded. I spent the majority of my time trying to heal him when I was sick myself. I'd love to keep it real. It was easier to deal with his issues than to deal with mine. I could safely work on him and not look at me.

One day I was on my knees praying and I began to cry unto God and told Him of the things that my husband was doing. I told Him that I was tired and I needed Him to fix my husband. But the thing I will never forget as long as I live is that God stopped me in my tracks and said, "I know what he is doing, but when are you going to tell me about you?" He said, "Joyce, I see him and know that he is broken, but do you realize that you are, too?" God said, "Joyce, what you don't understand is that I need to heal *you*. When are you going to tell me to make you keep your mouth closed and let me fight this battle? When are you going to tell me to make you a virtuous woman of God? When will you ask me to heal you from your past and your pain?" He said, "Although your husband needs to be delivered, so do you!"

God has a way of making us face the very things we are hiding from! Now, many years later, I understand that God was using my husband to make me look at myself in the mirror and face *me*. Had it not been for my relationship with my husband, I would have never seen how wounded I was. I had anger and bitterness in me that I would have never seen. If I had not identified the brokenness in him, I would have never seen it in myself. What I couldn't see was I was married to a wonderful, genuinely good-hearted but broken man who did not understand and properly handle his pain and the pressure it brought with it — and neither did I. We were both self-medicating.

There were days when his actions to his addiction looked just like my response to my pain. Where my husband used crack cocaine to escape his painful reality, I used comfort food. We were both hurting. His drug addiction took him out of the house, but my pain held me prisoner inside the house. My jail cell was my kitchen and the warden was food! Within me it became my pacifier — it brought me comfort through it all. Seeing my husband helped me identify the place where I had hidden for the majority of my life. My husband's pain caused me to see my own scars and helped me identify how I handled and processed my pain.

I grew up in a dysfunctional household. My parents bickered and argued. My mother and father would always make sure that we had everything we needed, even though they didn't realize what we needed was a peaceful environment more than anything. So, they kept us in a war zone oftentimes. Unfortunately, we had to choose sides and that was unfair to us as children. My room and my food became safe things for me. When I became overwhelmed, I chose food for comfort.

There were days when I would sit down and tell my husband that we were both struggling with an addiction. I would say you are fighting cocaine, but I am fighting food. Your escape is the streets and drugs that you use, but my escape is the junk food I consume. Am I still in the fight? Yes. Am I winning the battle? Yes. But some days more than others. How can I lose when I am on the winning team? It is Christ who gives me victory. That is why I am confident that I am a winner and that is all I need to know!

I want you to know that these behaviors did not show up in my marriage — they were there *before* I married my husband. And the reason I did not see it before was because of the environment that I lived in. The life I was living with my husband mirrored the life I had lived all of my childhood and my adult life. With him I created an atmosphere that reflected my past experiences, and those experiences were disorder and pain. So, our marriage became a response to my painful environment. It was not peace that I pursued, it was pandemonium because that was what I was accustomed to. There were times I recall my husband telling me that I enjoyed arguing because that was the environment I was raised in. To him arguing was not normal; to me what I was experiencing was my normal.

Boy...I say this while fighting back the tears. But I must take a moment to stop and thank a very dear friend of mine who did not allow me to stay in the prison I was in. God works in mysterious ways. He used my pastor, Bishop Brehon L. Hall. He could see the hurt in me and he would not let me settle for a life of chaos.

There were times I thought his methods were confusing and very painful, but what I came to realize was that it was not Pastor Hall at work

— it was God. Because of my obedience to God and my dear Father understanding that I would obey Him even if it would cause me great pain, God placed me in an environment and demanded that I stay until I could see the real core of who I am.

He placed me in an environment where I would not be allowed to take care of others — I was forced to take care of me. My loving Father took away my crutches and all of my excuses. It was then that I realized I had come full circle and I was forced to see me. The people I had elected to be my life's assignment were taken. And I had no one to care for but myself. God took my husband, my father, and last, my mother. And upon doing that He then sent me to a man of God who would push me indirectly to fight for the inner me.

The ministry that God strategically placed me in was completely different from any I had been in before. I came from a culture and environment where I had access to my leaders, but with the bishop it was not so freely given, which meant I had to grow up and figure things out on my own.

I was forced to rely on God for the answers and allow the Word that was ministered to me over the dais to find and heal me. God had boxed me in. He was forcing me to fight whether I wanted to or not. God took me to the center core of the battle and threw me in, and said, "Fight if you want to survive!" I was charting unfamiliar territory and surroundings, and that territory was claimed.

It was confusing because it left me with no one to save but me. What I understand now is what I was fighting for was inner peace. When I look at it now, the majority of my life had been centered on me rescuing others. That is why I was fighting the process, and it was the process that would bring to me the healing. There was no one at that point in my life for me to save but me. And where I was passive and hiding from my insecurities, I now had to learn to fight if I wanted to survive.

God used Bishop Hall to tell me that all of my life I had lived in chaos and I didn't understand what peace was. He was trying to help me find a place of peace and live in it. The process was painful and oftentimes lonely, not to mention that I cried many a night. But it made me fight to discover more of who I am. And now that I understand myself better, I will never compare myself to others again. Like I said, I didn't like the process, but it made me believe in me. Not only did it make me believe in me, but it made me believe in the God that is in me even more. It strengthened my faith.

What I couldn't see was I had been trying to save people all of my life. I was codependent and that is what codependent people do. We become passive, accepting and tolerating the inappropriate behavior of others so that we can't really see the hurt within ourselves. We feel the need to rescue others when we are drowning in our own pain.

Codependent people struggle with low self-esteem and their own identities. That is why they are willing to accept abusive relationships — because of their lack of confidence and lack of ability to believe in who they are. They walk every day of their lives feeling inferior to others, allowing other people to establish their standard of self-worth. And because they cannot see their worth, they are willing to become surrogate mothers and fathers to people suffering from painful issues.

Codependent persons allow these dependent people to escape responsibility for their bad choices. They refuse to hold the dependent person accountable, and this action hinders the dependent person from maturing. When we search out codependent patterns, it appears that they find it much easier to care for the needs of others than to focus on their own. Why fix myself when I can spend my life fixing you? And the reason is your baggage is a lot easier to carry than mine. My issues require me to dig deeper and the pain and chaos that I would have to deal with is much, much more intense. So, codependent people settle for the lesser of the two evils. This places them in the position of savior, and in turn their knight-in-shining-armor action releases the dependent personality from its responsibility to achieve and grow. In doing so, they never have to face their hardcore issues as long as the codependent person or persons are there to save them. These relationships are always one-sided. The addict is always taking, and the codependent person is always giving.

Codependent people repress their emotions and their needs. They develop behaviors that help them deny, ignore, or avoid difficult emotions. They are good at detaching themselves. They will shut down and not talk. They don't touch. They don't confront. They don't feel. And one of the biggest things is they don't trust. Not only do they not trust others, they don't trust themselves.

That is why I say it was easier to save my

husband than it was to save me. I require a lot of work. Have I made it yet? No. But am I on my way? Yes. To be very honest with you, I still have great issues and fears that I face on a day-to-day basis, but I continue to fight with the power of God. What I understand now is that there are layers of pain, abuse, and offenses that God is stripping off of me. And that is not something that can be completed overnight. It is a process. But at this period in my life, at least I am willing to stand still and let God get the job done.

I was in a mess, but thanks be to God who gives to us the victory. The things that were hidden and covered up have now come out into the open. I can see life through another lens. My life is not perfect, but it is no longer in the state of chaos that it once was in. God has healed some broken places in my heart because I desired to forgive and let go. God is repairing the cracks in my clay pot, and I really don't see things the way I used to. Forgiveness is so powerful that it will force you to look at yourself even when you don't want to. It will cause you to stop the cover-up.

Let's stop and pray:

Father, in the name of Jesus, thank You for opening the eyes of our understanding and allowing us to see ourselves, even if seeing hurts. We realize that all things are working together for the good of those who love You and are called according to Your purpose. Thank You, Lord, for Your wisdom and letting us experience some uncomfortable places in life. These tight places stretch and cause us to become the children that You will be well-pleased with. God, I want to thank You for forcing us to stand face-to-face with our destiny and identify who we really are. Thank You for uncovering all of our hidden pain and forcing us to deal with it. I love You, Lord, because You challenge us to fight for who we are to become by stripping off the mask that we are parading around in. And after You have taken our mask from us, You reveal to us the true essence of who You have created us to be. Daddy, You are so amazing and awesome. I love You with my whole heart, mind, body, and soul. Thank You, Lord, for choosing me to be one of Your children. I am so thankful.

Love You, Father. I am just grateful in the name of Jesus Christ.

Amen

Chapter Eleven
No Hurt Like Church Hurt! Tamar Came to Serve

This is a chapter that everybody who has ever been in church for any length of time can identify with. There is no hurt like church hurt. I had never been so badly wounded than I was when I came to my Father's house! I felt like David when he said in *Psalm 55:12-14 — For it was not an enemy that reproached me; then I could have borne it: neither was it he that hated me that did magnify himself against me; then I would have hid myself from him: [13] But it was thou, a man mine equal, my guide, and mine acquaintance. [14] We took sweet counsel together, and walked unto the house of God in company.*

David was agonizing over the fact that it was not his enemy causing him grief (because he said he could have borne it), but it was his friend. It is one thing to be betrayed by an enemy; it is another to be betrayed by a friend. When you look at and compare a friend to an enemy, you see that a friend is someone you can trust and rely on — a person you are emotionally attached to. They are your comrade; a fellow soldier, someone who will fight with you and for you, a friend who will partner with you. He or she is someone who is involved in your everyday activities; they are a part of your life. They are there for you when you need them and they will walk with you through life's difficult times. Friends share in your joy and they share in your grief.

That is why we read in Psalms about the distress of David. He was speaking of a person or persons very closely associated to him and they had greatly betrayed him. How painful can that be?

When something like this happens, there is really no pain you can compare it to. That is why David said had it been an enemy, he could have taken it, because you expect an enemy to treat you cruelly. But when it comes from someone you love and respect, it is a horse of a different color.

The psalmist continues to convey to us that it was not the one who hated him that magnified himself against him, because he said he could have hidden. When you have a hater, you know just how to treat them. With someone who hates you, you anticipate or expect them to be deceiving and vindictive. It is obvious that they detest and despise you. It is in your nature to stay on guard and stay alert. You foresee them doing something evil to try to frustrate and destroy you. But when you don't suspect that they are even thinking or plotting wickedness against you, it leaves you unprepared for the offense. There is a saying that says you should keep your friends close but keep your enemies closer.

When we look at David further, the text identifies this person as his equal. It was a person who was very similar to him. There was nothing strange about this individual; the both of them had everything in common. This friend had the same values and qualities as David. He had the same rights, status, and opportunities that David possessed. Have you ever been wounded by someone who really didn't have any reason to come against you? They were just as successful as you were and as gifted as you were, yet they still turned on you — and you thought that the both of you were cool. As I always say — my, my, my, my, my.

Another thing that the scripture reveals to us is this person was David's guide. David was close enough to this person to share information, and this individual was giving him instructions. I believe the most hurtful thing about all of this is that David said this person was his acquaintance and they took sweet counsel together. This was a friend who David shared his intimate secrets with. They discussed the things that were going on in each other's lives. If I must be betrayed, please don't let it be by the one that I have poured my heart and soul out to. It is very painful to think that the person you trusted with your most intimate secrets is the same person who places the knife in your back. It is like an unexplained death that only God can heal.

Then the text says that they walked unto the house of God. David was with a person who shared his faith and they trusted in the same God. Look at the scriptures — they went to church together. Don't take my word for it — read it for yourself. It said they walked unto the house of God in company. They came to church together! They sat on the same pew right next to each other! They slapped each other high-fives when the sermon was good! They heard the same messages. This pain did not come from the enemy or an ungodly person; it came from a church friend! This was someone who worshipped and shared David's same beliefs. I can deal with the pain of an enemy, but when we say that we love the same God and we are to be like Him, then we treat each other like strangers and enemies, we have a problem! There is no hurt like church hurt! This is because we are supposed to be in the same family. We should have the same DNA, and that DNA is the blood of Jesus. And because we are part of the same bloodline, we should have the same traits as our Father. Yet, we still wound and hurt each other. Something is seriously wrong with this picture!

Even David's daughter Tamar could testify to the pain and agony of betrayal by someone she loved and respected. The closeness of their relationship can identify the intensity of their pain. Tamar and Amnon were sister and brother. They are a reflection of who we are in the body of Christ. Because they were brother and sister, they were not supposed to be enemies. Neither of them should have been plotting nor scheming against each other. The reality is they had a bond and a connection through their father, just as we have a bond and a connection through our Lord and Savior Jesus Christ. But as this story depicts, there was a line crossed and it caused the violation of an innocent victim, which was Tamar.

We often cross multiple lines in the body of Christ. We fail to remember that we are to have compassion and love for each other. There has to be a greater degree of respect, concern, and accountability in the house of God. We cannot continue to violate one another and offend our sisters and brothers — or anyone for that matter — especially if we say we love God!

God expects His children to have love and compassion for His creation, even when we don't feel that we can. We tend to think that this applies only to the house of God and that we should love only God's children. But in reality, we should show more love outside of the house of God so that we can, with our love, win over the unbeliever.

We should be diligent in showing the love of Christ at all times, even if the times make it hard for us to reveal His love. And the reason is, during these difficult moments that is when God gets the greatest glory. It is during the course of those times that you completely understand that it is not in your ability to love, but you are given a genuine love by the grace of God, and the love you are given is God's love.

So, that is why, when I get to this part of the story about Tamar and her brother Amnon, I find it to be so extremely heartbreaking because Tamar came out of obedience to her father, and **she just came to serve!** Look at what the scripture says in *2 Samuel 13:7 — Then David sent home to Tamar, saying, Go now to thy brother Amnon's house, and dress him meat.* How many children of God have come to the house of God because our Heavenly Father told us to come? The only reason that we are in God's house is because He sent us!

I want you to hear me and hear me clearly. Everyone — and I mean *everyone* — who is called of God has a duty and a responsibility as a child of God to build and strengthen God's Kingdom here on earth. There is an assignment on your life whether you want to believe it or not. And it is God who sends you to the place to fulfill your assignment. He attaches you to a ministry and a leader. He tells you what town, city, state, region or country to work in. God orchestrates all of the fine details, and we just follow and obey. That is why, in the process of obeying God, I am sure that you never thought in your wildest dreams that you would become as hurt and broken by the people that you came to serve. Just thinking about it requires another "my, my, my, my, my" moment.

When we look closely and compare the events surrounding Tamar to the atmosphere of the church, we see that she went to attend to the needs of her brother and what she got in return was appalling. Out of obedience to her father, Tamar was placed in a situation where she received great pain — all because she was willing to fulfill her father's demand and attend to Amnon's needs.

I want every reader to understand that following God is not easy, but what God will do is give you the grace and strength to get the job done. Following God will place you in many painful situations, but the end result is these painful places will give you the greatest benefit. They cause you to seek after God like never before. Paul said in *Philip. 3:10 — That I may know him, and the power of his resurrection, and the fellowship of his sufferings, being made conformable unto his death.* It is our pain and our suffering that gives us an opportunity to know God.

We must learn to completely trust our Father and believe that no matter what position or place He calls us to fulfill in this life, with our whole heart, mind, body, and soul we must believe that He would never position us in a place that would completely destroy us. That is the reason Tamar went to her brother Amnon's house in complete confidence that her father's love would never place her in harm's way. I am sure that you could never make Tamar believe that her father would knowingly place her in a position that would strip her of her femininity and her virginity, or even allow her to experience the rejection that she did by the hands of her own brother, Amnon.

Take note of the precious gift that Amnon stole from Tamar. Amnon did not just violate Tamar, but he defiled the threshold that God had prepared for her so that one day Tamar would be able to give birth. This is the place where dreams are birthed, destinies are created, visions are perceived, and purpose is brought forth.

That is why it is so important that we, as children of God, do not allow the wrong person to make a deposit into our spiritual womb. It contaminates the gateway to your soul. It leaves a filthy environment for the consummation of God, because it is only in a purified womb that God can leave a genuine deposit. That is why it is written in *1 Peter 1:16 — Because it is written, be ye holy; for I am holy*. It is God's desire to fill you to capacity with purpose, but in order for Him to plant the seed, He must know that you have surrendered all of you over to Him — and not only all of you, but all of who you ever hope to become.

So you see, Amnon desecrated the passage of conception that was only intended to be accessible by two individuals who were willing to give up their individual wills and come into one covenant together, and that covenant is marriage. In that one act, Amnon stripped her of something that she could never recover. That is what he stole from Tamar. Her brother stole her innocence, her future, her dreams, and her God-given purpose, and left behind a fragmented, rejected, wounded, and sexually abused young lady.

When you see this awful picture, you see a special gift that God has given to Tamar taken away by the hands of a selfish man. Women, your virginity is the one gift that your Heavenly Father gives you to give to the one special man that you love. He only gave this gift to his daughters — not his sons. Your virginity is your one unique treasure. It was designed by God just for you to have on your wedding day as a dowry to give to the man you love and you have chosen to submit your will to. And this gift was exclusively placed inside of you for him. Do you see the beautiful picture of love that is painted? It was given to you by the hands of Abba, our Heavenly Father. Oh my, what a display of a Father's love for His daughters! And you only have one opportunity to give it away. Once the package is open, it can never be resealed. So, choose wisely and very carefully who you feel is worthy to open your gift from God! It is the only dowry that you have to give to your husband in the covenant of marriage that came straight from Heaven and from the hands of God.

When you marry the man of your dreams, you can either enter into your union with the one gift from God that you chose to save for your husband, or you can enter into your marriage with memories of a series of ungodly intimate deposits from relationships that were never meant to last. And somewhere lost in the scheme of events you were either forced to, or you just simply gave away your virginity to someone who was not deserving of your love or your gift! Think about it. Which will you choose?

A woman's virginity is her signet. It is an emblem of her chaste and virtuous conduct. It reveals that she has saved herself for the man she will fall in love with. This is the gift that many women dream of giving to their husbands on their wedding night. No woman ever wants to be forced to spend her first intimate sexual encounter with a man she has not consented to surrender her virginity to — and especially not a relative. Place yourself in Tamar's shoes. What an awful picture to remember. Tamar would always remember that she was forced to relinquish her virginity to her brother.

It saddens me to think of the effects this one selfish act of rape likely caused. For the rest of her life Tamar would live with a lasting scar of brokenness. This one rape would paint in the mind of Tamar a canvas of regrettable pain and agony that she would be forced to remember for as long as she lived. And to add insult to injury, this was her brother committing the violation! This sexual abuse was not done by an acquaintance; rather, it was by someone she trusted and loved.

Tamar was moved by her love for her brother and her obedience to her father's command. This one act of submission would forever change her life. She found herself in a place where a conspiracy would be played out that would crush and destroy the very essence of her being. Her unrestricted love and obedience placed her in a place to be severely broken. It was Tamar who made the greatest sacrifice that day. She was stripped and wounded beyond repair. Her future and all of her dreams were altered by the hands of one man and his selfish, lustful desires. The cruelest part of this story is that Tamar was hurt by someone she was trying to help!

How many times have you been hurt by the ones you were trying to help? There is no hurt any greater than that. You try to help your friends and family, and they turn on you. You give yourself over to the care of your children, and they disrespect you. You are supporting your spouse, and they neglect you. Even at your job and in the community you feel a degree of rejection and pain for the loyalty that you display.

How many Tamars do we have in our churches, our homes, and in our societies? We live in a world where more people are takers and not givers. It is a sad place to live in when the only thing you can look forward to is being surrounded by people who are constantly taking. What kind of world are we really living in?

The saddest thing about all of this is we are sitting with our eyes closed, knowing that it is happening among our ministries. The most disheartening thing that I have ever seen is this behavior in the house of God. It is sad because Abba's house is supposed to be a place of comfort and healing! The place where we should find peace has become a place of pain, and I would love to know why! I keep hammering on this issue because Abba's house should be a place of rest, peace, and love! If there is anywhere in the world that I should be able to find healing, it should be in the house of God!

Men and women of God, we cannot continue the cover-up! The pain is real, the issues we struggle with are real, and the enemies that we war against are very real. But the power of God and the cross of Calvary are far greater than what we face and see. We just have to pick up our weapons and fight until there is no breath left within us. There must be a turnaround because our families, communities, and our world are what we are losing!

We want them to come and be a part of the body of believers, but look at how we treat these Tamars when they get to our ministries. Some of these Tamars come to serve and some come to be healed...yet they come. But when they come offering their gifts with the spirit of humility, we mishandle them and leave them wounded, frustrated, rejected, and brokenhearted. I am sure if they had known the treatment they would receive, they would have never consented to show up at all. Many of our sisters and brothers are saying, "I didn't come here for this!"

What do you do when God sends you to a place to worship, and when you get there you discover that you are not accepted? Do you leave or do you stay? If you really love God, you learn to serve in difficult places. And these places become the fertile ground upon which to build your relationship — not with man, but to build your relationship with God. Thank God that it is He who shields and protects you in these awful situations.

Yes, it is very disappointing and extremely disheartening because you come in looking to be used by God with a sincere heart, then you discover that the environment is cold and uninviting. The first thing you think is, *Is this really the church, because I was treated better than this in the streets.* Yet, we say this is God's house. Church, what are we going to do? Do we ignore these behaviors and act like these problems are not in the house of God? Or do we confront them head-on and seek change?

That is why I continue to say that these Tamars come to some of our sanctuaries with hopes of bringing to the body of Christ their gifts, talents, and abilities, but leave spiritually raped, emotionally drained, and stripped of their dignity, and their hunger for life and God. The only reason they are here is because of the call of a loving and caring Father. He gave them instructions to serve the brethren. But when they arrive they are met by people that possess cruel spirits of rejection, jealousy, and envy. These individuals have pre-determined plans to smother every gift and ability that these innocent Tamars have. They are bullied by insecure and jealous individuals.

Many of our Tamars are coming in, willing to give all that they have to the body of Christ. Their hearts and their spiritual postures say "just let me serve." They are crying, "Where can I be effective in the Kingdom of God?" Yet, what they receive are the ungodly antics of selfish ministries that offer them spiritual rejection. They are seduced by manipulation, spirits of control, jealousy, hatred, unforgiveness, and sexual deception. Many leaders take these Tamars and prostitute their gifts and callings in order to satisfy their own ungodly agendas.

These Tamars come to our churches eager to work. But because we have our social cliques, they never find a place to fit in or effectively give of their services. They are the ones who become the target because many feel like they might be their replacement, not realizing that our Father sent them there because of His love for His other children. Tamar has come to help the body of Christ become so much better. These Tamars never come to take away — they are sent to heal and serve.

We, as the body of Christ, must learn that there is enough work for everyone in the Kingdom. We must not become selfish in our approach to the new people that God has sent to the Kingdom. We must learn to embrace their gifts, talents, and abilities. We must learn to accept each person as a precious gift from God, knowing that they are given to the body of Christ to continue to help build His Kingdom. They are not sent to *subtract* — they are sent to *add*.

Body of Christ, give our Tamars a chance to present to our ministries the gifts that they come bearing. Let them come in and minister to the needs of God's people, unrestricted. Give them the freedom to find the peace and security that they need in the house of God. In our Father's house we don't need more takers, we need more givers. The Tamars are the givers, and the Amnons are the takers. Correctly identify who these Tamars are, release the yokes you have placed upon them, and let them serve with the spirit of freedom and not the spirit of fear. Because there is no hurt like church hurt!

Let's pray:

Father, in the name of Jesus, forgive us for mishandling the gifts that You have sent to our ministries. Lord, we are sorry. Give us Your wisdom and Your clear understanding on how to effectively use every child of God who enters into our doors. Let us not take their gifts and use them for our selfish agendas, but allow us to present them to the body of Christ to build and edify Your Kingdom. Lord, there are so many things that we don't yet understand, but it is not our desire to wound, hurt, or offend. Search our hearts and our minds, and remove any selfish and lustful desires from us now. We want to greatly please You and do only the things that are pleasing in Your sight. Don't let us hurt our sisters and brothers who come to Your house to serve and leave them worse off than when they came. Give each and every one of us the heart of a servant. Teach us to have the spirit of humility. Let it continue to be a part of our Godly nature. It is our most humble desire to live this life so that one day we can live it in eternity with You forever. Show us the ways of righteousness and give us the heart and mind to obey Your loving Word.

We love You, dear Father. These things we ask in the name of Jesus Christ.

Amen

Chapter Twelve
Keep Fighting and Believing

*W*e are coming to the close of these scriptures and the depiction of the very painful experience of Tamar's. We see that there was a great conspiracy by her brother Amnon given under the instruction of his friend, Jonadab. Once the wheels of wickedness began to turn, they turned swiftly. Take note of the events that led up to the actual rape and look at the subtle way that Amnon cunningly violated Tamar.

The bible says that Amnon refused to be served in the presence of others. He gives a command that every man leave their presence. *2 Samuel 13:9 — And she took a pan, and poured them out before him; but he refused to eat. And Amnon said, Have out all men from me. And they went out every man from him.* Now Tamar is the only one left in his quarters. When everyone Tamar could rely on to witness, defend, or protect her was gone, her brother cunningly began to unfold his evil plan. Amnon was strategically setting Tamar up for the kill. Check out the coward.

The next thing he did was call her to his bed chambers, just like a hunter would corner his prey. Now he was ready for the kill. Look at the innocence of Tamar and her willingness to serve, never considering the danger that was awaiting her. She entered into her brother's bed chamber, preparing to supply him with the needed meal to lift his countenance. Yet, she found herself caged in like an animal, being attacked at the hands of the one she served and loved.

Have you ever gone to serve, and the very act of kindness that should have given you a sense of fulfillment and joy has now become your place of pain, violation, and rejection? The caring gestures of love, faithfulness, and commitment have suddenly become a battleground where you fight to maintain your peace, self-respect, and dignity. The ones who should be displaying gratitude for your acts of compassion and generosity are the ones plotting to take everything that is of any value to you.

The acts of thoughtfulness that you were willing to extend to your loved ones, which were meant to bring them joy, have now become the catalyst to bring you sorrow. More times than imagined, the ones you are trying to love are the ones who have placed you in the greatest position of pain. Countless times they are the ones you have tried to protect and defend. Your care for them has become your life investment. You have spent the majority of your whole life making sure they have everything that they need or desire. Over and over again you have neglected your needs to ensure that theirs were successfully met. As I said in the previous chapter, it is not your enemy, but it is the one you have placed as your heart's desire to care for, love and serve. Understand that even though your love ones are the instruments that are used to apply the pain, there still is a greater force behind the scene.

You have to know that it is more detailed

than what you can see and comprehend. There is a mastermind and it is Satan. He will go to great lengths to destroy you. Satan is very patient and his kingdom is very organized and unified. It is no problem for him to wait. He will wait for as long as it takes to strip you of every promise that God has made to you. And I mean, he will wait years. And not only years, if it takes a lifetime he will patiently wait. He hangs around until you have gotten weary and tired in the fight. He always executes his plan when you are not watching and praying, and that is when that old slick serpent springs the trap. He knows it is at these instances that you are blind to his crafty moves.

My sisters and brothers, you have to stay on a diligent watch for your adversary, the Devil, because he has been studying you and your family for generations. He knows the times and the seasons to send the assassins to destroy you. He is aware of what will work and what will not work. That Devil has you and your whole family figured out. He knows what man to send to you and when to send him. Satan knows if you like them tall, dark, and handsome, or white, light, and bright. Guess what? He has them measured to size just for you. And gentlemen, he knows what woman to present and he understands exactly how to wrap her. Satan will flaunt her before you in an exquisite package. Making her tailor-made just for you — 36-24-36. And if that won't work, he is like the train porter who shouts, "Pop corn, peanuts, potato chips!" and if that won't work, "Candy, gum, soda!" That Devil will keep presenting things until he finds the things you will accept. Believe you me, he knows what you like and dislike, and he has a bag full of tricks.

You might not want to believe it, but the enemy has been setting traps for you to fall into all of your life. He has studied your weak areas because he was the one who set the trap that broke your confidence. He caused you to stop believing in you, and believing in the wonderful things that God said about you. He was the one who prevented you from dreaming. He told you the lie that God didn't want you and couldn't use you. He stopped you from seeing everything that God has invested in you. As a matter of fact, he has been setting traps for your family for generations.

Look at the basic patterns of your family structure and see if you don't see generational behaviors. Well, guess who is behind it all? If you said Satan, then you have guessed right! Can't you see just as God has divinely ordered your steps to greatness, Satan has strategically caused you to stumble in darkness, leaving you uncertain of your future.

Let's expose the game, because he has been playing games with your mind for years. Didn't you know Satan is the one who continues to suggest to you that you are a failure and no one will like you or understand you? Haven't you figured out yet that it is Satan who continues to point out to you all of your weak and blind spots? Have you stopped to wonder why, when you are at the peak of success, he reminds you of your failures? He has caused you to tap into every evil thing that will redirect your heart and your mind, causing you to lose sight of God and your God-given ability to become productive, peaceful, and successful.

God declares that you are more than a conqueror in Christ Jesus. God says that you can do all things through He who loves you. But Satan bellows in your ears, telling you that you can never make it! You are wasting time. Why try, anyway? You will never fit in. They won't want or believe you, anyway. What's the use — just give up! You know that you are a big failure and no one cares. You are not smart enough — you know that you always quit. Did God tell you to do that, anyway?

These cunning devices are crafted to suggest failure. Satan has them in his arsenal of weapons ready to be used to take you out. They are the ones designed to maim and cripple your ability to reach your full potential in God and in life. That is why he corners you, isolates you, so he can cause you to have a victim mentality. He leaves you with feelings of inferiority and insecurity, completely rejected and totally unwanted. If that is you, guess what? You have been spiritually raped by the Devil and his imps.

But wait one minute. I must add a disclaimer to this, because it is not always the satanic forces of darkness at work. We can do a pretty good job at killing our dreams ourselves. Our fleshly desires can blind us to the things God has in store for us. This happens when we see ourselves through the eyes of our own ability and not through the lens of our Creator, which is God. Seeing our destiny and future through our view leaves us seeing only part of the overall picture. But when we look at it through the eyes of God, we can see it from beginning to end. He knows it all, which is why we must trust God to give to us the full scope of His God-given plans for our lives.

It takes Satan to suggest to us our failures, but we have to sign the check and accept the package. It is not the suggestion that causes the damage; it is when we endorse it. We must learn not to fund another man's plan that conjures up or implies defeat for our lives — or should I say another *Devil's* plan? When you come into agreement with the enemy — and that enemy might even be you — then you have given them the resources to create an environment of failure for you to battle for the rest of your life.

Good God Almighty. I cancel every written check in the spirit that I have endorsed for the enemy. I seize every account that will give him access to my destiny, my future, my children's future, and every generation to come. I dry up bank accounts, IRAs, annuities, and investments in the world of darkness where the enemies have controlled and locked down my flow of abundance, joy, and peace. I transfer everything into the Kingdom of God and place a demand in the spirit that my riches be released. I now have full access to the prosperity of God and my barns will overflow with wealth, joy, peace, love, and contentment. I command it in the name of our Lord and Savior, Jesus Christ. Amen. (We needed a prayer break right there! Whew, oh yes we did!)

Now, let's get back to business, because we have a few more corners to turn before we get to the end. That is why we must faithfully and diligently watch, as well as pray, because when he devises a plan, and if it takes him years to get it accomplished, then he will patiently wait until it is successfully executed. The only thing that the enemy needs is for you to buy into the lie! All of your life the enemy has been waiting to get you in the right position to kill, steal, rob, and destroy you. He takes advantage of the weak and feeble areas of your character. As I have said before, he studies his victims and he knows you and your family inside out. Believe you me, he has homed in on every flaw that you have and he knows how much pressure to apply to get you to break. But thanks be to God who gives to us the victory every time. We do have a hero and he has defeated our sinister enemy.

That is why the story of Tamar and Amnon seems so sad, because it leaves a trail of pain, bitterness, and hatred. A virgin is crushed and seriously wounded. This is not a fairytale; these are the events of a real family that experienced real pain from the hands of one they should have been able to trust. *2 Samuel 13:10-14 — And Amnon said unto Tamar Bring the meat into the chamber that I may eat of thine hand. And Tamar took the cakes which she had made, and brought them into the chamber to Amnon her brother. [11] And when she had brought them unto him to eat, he took hold of her, and said unto her, Come lie with me, my sister. [12] And she answered him, Nay, my brother; do not force me; for no such thing ought to be done in Israel: do not thou this folly. [13] And I, whither shall I cause my shame to go? And as for thee, thou shalt be as one of the fools in Israel. Now therefore, I pray thee, speak unto the king; for he will not withhold me from thee. [14] Howbeit he would not hearken unto her voice: but, being stronger than she, forced her, and lay with her.* Amnon asked her to bring to him what she had prepared, and the only way that he would receive it was in private. Now she was isolated and secluded.

Will you, the reader, for just a moment, allow me a random thought? I often wonder why it is that when we are going through the most difficult times of our lives, the first thing that happens is we find ourselves alone or desiring to be alone. Is it possible that there is a connection with trouble, pain, and despair? And do these emotions automatically lead us to desire to be alone? Do these feelings motivate us to disconnect from others, or do they push others to disconnect from us? Regardless, when we experience pain, rejection, frustration, and any-thing that causes discomfort, many times we will automatically find ourselves positioned alone and feeling helpless.

When you take a close look at the events, you will see that oftentimes it is during these painful seasons that we feel that God has left us and we are standing on our own. It amazes me. And oh yes, I must be real — I am guilty of this behavior. The first thing I desire to do when I am hurting is close everyone out and be by myself. And the funny thing is it becomes a vicious, painful circle. When I am alone, things seem to close in even more. So what I realize is it hurts to be alone, yet it hurts to be in the presence of others also, so it is like a no-win situation.

That is why when we find ourselves feeling

this way, we must fight to stay connected to others. The bible lets us know that there is strength in numbers. Regardless of how I feel, I need my sisters and brothers, friends, family, and coworkers to maintain a sense of sanity, especially when I am facing difficult times. I want to encourage you to stay connected to someone in the times of testing and trouble. I just thought I would drop that thought in to get you to think about the danger of separating yourself when faced with trouble.

Even though we withdraw because of our pain, I am not referring to voluntary, painful withdrawal; I am speaking about the cunning trick of removing everyone and everything from an individual so that they can become a victim. No, it is not good to be alone, but it is even worse when you are forced into a place of seclusion. This is the oldest trick in the book and it is an old war tactic. The Devil is very skillful at using it. He has defeated great men and women by dividing and conquering. As a matter of fact, not only has he destroyed men and women, but he has brought down empires.

The game of isolation is a smooth and sneaky game, and you see this behavior instinctively displayed in animals. It is a built-in mechanism designed to cut prey off from the pack and completely devour and destroy them. In the animal kingdom it is called the way of the food chain. It is sad that we, being humans, can act just like animals.

In the animal world, the animals usually selected to become targets are very young, very old, very sick, or not paying attention to their surroundings. Their predators watch to see who displays signs of weakness and they cut that selected animal completely off from everyone else. They are skillful at spotting the weakest member of the clan and separating them from the horde. It is natural for the stronger to take advantage of those that are weak and sickly.

Can't you see this in the depiction of the events with Tamar and Amnon? He is the stronger, dominant one. Poor Tamar is the prey and Amnon is the hunter. The animal's predatory instincts find a way to corner their prey, leaving them nowhere to go and with no one to help them. Sounds like the events to this story, doesn't it? Look at what it does. It places the animal in a vulnerable position of weakness. Again, I say it sounds like the fate of Tamar. Don't you remember in scripture how Amnon studied Tamar until he became sick? The plan to lay with Tamar did not come into fruition overnight. He had watched her when she didn't know that he was looking or even desiring her. Sounds like animal instinct to me.

This story reminds me of an old song written by George Clinton called "The Atomic Dog." A few of the lyrics state "like the boys when they're out there walkin' the streets may compete, but nothing but the dog in ya ruff, ruff, ruff. Why must I feel like that? Why must I chase the cat, nothing but the dog in ya." Whether you want to believe it or not, when we closely search out the facts of this story, we see that it is nothing but the Devil in Amnon, and his lustful flesh plotting to take advantage of his sister, Tamar.

Note that this method of seclusion and

isolation is very effective in conquering anything. When the enemy can get you by yourself and alone, he can take total advantage of you. Check out what *Eccles. 4:9-10* says. ***Two are better than one; because they have a good reward for their labour. [10] For if they fall, the one will lift up his fellow: but woe to him that is alone when he falleth; for he hath not another to help him up.*** Solomon, a man of great wisdom, tells us woe to him that falls alone because no one is there to lift him up. But he says two is always better than one, because if he falls then there is someone to pick him up. So, now can you clearly see why Amnon placed his sister Tamar in an isolated position?

Just as the frail, unsuspecting victims in the animal kingdom, I am sure that Tamar never sensed the danger that she was in. It probably never crossed her mind that someone she was being so attentive to would ever bring her that type of harm. Even after the men left I am sure that Tamar never considered that she would become a party to the cruel display of abuse. I have to believe that once she realized the full impact of her brother's awful plan, then every emotion she possessed was in absolute despair.

As soon as you come to the realization that you are secluded and isolated with someone who has presented qualities of an assailant, it has a tendency to leave you feeling weakened, powerless, and defeated. Standing alone in an unhealthy and threatening environment brings with it feelings of rejection, fear, frustration, inferiority, isolation, exclusion, and powerlessness.

It is like standing in zero-degree weather,

hoping that the cold will go away, praying for a safe place to take refuge. Your mind is frantically searching for a place to avoid the horror of the circumstance. You are seeking an environment of serenity and calm because your situation is displaying signs of disaster. Frenetically, you search for an escape route that affords you the shelter of comfort and security, because what you are in the middle of is a hostile ambiance that is cold and uninviting.

I don't care what you think; for me the worst place to be is in a position alone with an enemy or a deceiver. No matter what you do or say, no one is there to defend you or your position. The worst place for an abused wife to be is in a home with a violent and verbally abusive husband. The physical and verbal abuse leaves her powerless and defenseless to fight off the physical, mental, and emotional attacks. You ask the question, "Who is there to defend me when I am cornered and secluded? Who will fight with me and for me?" My sisters and my brothers, please always try to remember that there is an invisible force standing with you at all times. You have a heavenly host right by your side who will walk with you to the very end of your painful experience. And no matter what you find yourselves coming out of, you will always win if you don't give up in the middle of the fight.

Amnon knew the strategic move he needed to take to get what he desired. That is why Amnon placed Tamar in a situation where no one would be able to hear her screams or her cries. He positioned her in a perfect place to abuse her.

Have you ever been in a place where you were screaming for help, but no one was there to listen? You were so broken that you were screaming, but there was no sound coming out. You start out with a loud, boisterous scream of passion, then suddenly realize that you have been isolated by the enemy and there is no one listening to you or for you. Then your scream becomes a whisper, and your whisper becomes silent. And nobody understands why you are the way you are. They can't figure out why you have built the wall. It is because you have been spiritually, emotionally, and mentally raped. And it was all done behind closed doors and alone.

At this point, Amnon has played the game. He has moved all of his pieces in place and has strategically trapped his sister Tamar and it is checkmate. He has her right where he wants her. Poor Tamar is caged in like an animal. I am sure that Tamar, at this point, was uncertain of her plight, panic-stricken and full of fear and sorrow. I know she couldn't believe what was happening to her. And all of this was done by the hands of someone she should have been able to trust. After all, this was by her own flesh and blood.

Most individuals desire to trust the ones they love. There should be a certain amount of trust that we should be able to expect from our friends and families, and the people we work with and work for. And the reason that we cannot trust the people surrounding us is that we, as a society, have not learned to cultivate our environment with the right foundational principles and establish a solid respect for God. Once we are willing to follow the heart and mind of Christ, then and only then will we be able to trust our neighbors and the people in our communities. We must place God at center stage at all times.

When God is not center stage and we have not developed our relationships surrounding Him, our families, communities, and churches become targets to abusers. What has happened in our world is that there is so much ungodliness. The world as a whole has lost our God consciousness and we are doing everything that feels good and right to us. But what we fail to identify is what feels right to us is not always right for us. And when we find ourselves in these uncomfortable situations, we seek a safe place to retreat to. I believe that it is within our nature to try to find ways to protect the wounded places of our souls. We instinctively learn to guard our hearts, minds, and our emotions. And if we can't find a comfortable environment that we can trust for ourselves and the people we love, we begin to apply safety nets and escape mechanisms so that it will not leave us or our loved ones open to any other violators or predators. And sometimes the safety precautions we put in place can be as painful and decaying to us as what caused the offense.

The wrong safety nets can cause you to live behind walls and barricades that are unhealthy, unsafe, and very insecure. These ineffective walls might give you security from the things and the people from *without*, but the sad thing about a wall is it will not protect you from what is *within*.

Yes, you have locked everyone else out, but you have locked you in. And the things you are surrounded by in your fenced-in walls are your pain, rejection, insecurity, bitterness, hatred, and a ball of self-pity. So, everything you are doing to secure your safety could turn out to be just as destructive. You could be caught up in a catch-22 and not even know it. You might be left not fighting the offender — you might be left fighting *you!*

That is why this tragic story brings tears to my eyes. Looking at someone who should have been loved, accepted, and appreciated for their acts of kindness; who is now being taken advantage of...isn't it heartbreaking? Tamar was stripped of her virginity and it was all done without anyone there to intercede. Tamar was placed in a position where no one would be able to hear her scream or cry. Oh, how awfully sad that day must have been. It is like waking up out of a bad dream and thinking this just could not be happening — can someone please pinch me and wake me up? Have you ever been in a place where life left you gasping for air and things have gotten so out of control, and you feel like this can't be real? Can someone please shake me so I can escape all of this pain?

You are crushed and feeling defeated. There is a reservoir of disappointment coming out of your soul and you have become numb to your surroundings, and no one is there to hear your whimper or cry. You begin to wonder, who can I call or turn to? And for the first time you realize that you are alone. Oh, how sad it is to be violated and standing alone.

If you will allow me to believe and imagine, I know that Tamar was not alone on that horrible day — all of Heaven was watching with tear-stained eyes. God and the heavenly host was there healing and ministering to her broken places of despair. God took all of Tamar's tears and placed them in bottles as a memorial of her sacrifice for her obedient service to the one she loved. ***Psalm 56:8 — Thou hast taken account of my wanderings; Put my tears in Thy bottle; Are they not in Thy book?*** God saw her pain and He was taking notes. And as God took Tamar's tears and bottled them up, He is doing the same thing for all of the Tamars who are reading the pages of this book.

When you are faced with painful situations in your life, God will do the same thing for you. He knows and sees your disappointment and your pain. That is why I am writing this, to let you know. Don't get lost in your pain to the point that you don't know who you are. Please do not allow the cruel acts of others to turn your heart into anger, bitterness, and hatred. God is there to walk with you and even carry you through these tough times. Tamar was alone in a house with a man who would crush her dreams.

Being left alone in the hands of someone who is selfish and ready to violate you is more than anyone can stand. How many Tamars have been wounded in the pastor's office and in his secret counsel — made to feel less than inadequate and unneeded? These men and women of God are forced to fight to measure up to a standard that they can never reach or achieve because the leaders have already predetermined in their hearts that these Tamars will never fit into the ministry anyway, or they will never be good enough to get the job or promotion. They can never fit their qualifications or standards. They are not of the right ethnic group. And we see day after day that these cruel Amnons string these poor Tamars along. They tolerate them long enough to get from these poor Tamars what they need, want, and desire — using them and giving them just enough hope to believe that they really care. And they knew that there was always a hidden agenda from the start.

But the 33rd chapter of Ezekiel talks to the shepherd clearly. God gives a clear description of these false and ungodly men and women and He describes their outcome. I am not just talking about the church, although it is my main assignment at this time, but to anyone who has an advantage over someone else. If you are evil, selfish, and cruel to the meek and humble, then the anger of the Lord is against you. *Ezekiel 34:1-10* says, *Then the word of the Lord came to me saying, [2] "Son of man, prophesy against the shepherds of Israel. Prophesy and say to those shepherds, 'Thus says the Lord God, "Woe, shepherds of Israel who have been feeding themselves! Should not the shepherds feed the flock? [3] "You eat the fat and clothe yourselves with the wool; you slaughter the fat sheep without feeding the flock. [4] "Those who are sickly you have not strengthened, the diseased you have not healed, the broken you have not bound up, the scattered you have not brought back, nor have you sought for the lost; but with force and with severity you have dominated them. [5] "And they were scattered for lack of a shepherd, and they became food for every beast of the field and were scattered. [6] "My flock wandered through all the mountains and on every high hill, and my flock was scattered over all the surface of the earth; and there was no one to search or seek for them." ' "*

[7] Therefore, you shepherds, hear the word of the Lord: [8] "As I live," declares the Lord God, "surely because My flock has become a prey, My flock has even become food for all the beasts of the field for lack of a shepherd, and My shepherds did not search for My flock, but rather the shepherds fed themselves and did not feed My flock; [9] therefore, you shepherds, hear the word of the Lord: [10] 'Thus says the Lord God, "Behold, I am against the shepherds, and I shall demand My sheep from them and make them cease from feeding sheep. So the shepherds will not feed themselves anymore, but I shall deliver my flock from their mouth, that they may not be food for them."

If this is not you, then I am not talking to you, but just in case it is...stop pimping God's people! You might not want to believe it, but God is preparing judgment for the leaders that wound and hurt His sheep. Stop using innocent people to fulfill your lustful and greedy desires. What a sad day and time we live in. It is one thing to be raped in the world, but it is a whole new ballgame when we are raped in the church. Not only raped, but forced to commit spiritual incest by the hands of men and women who refer to their spiritual children as sons and daughters of the gospel. Many of these leaders are exploiting their sons' and daughters' weaknesses and their frailties in order to accomplish their selfish and ungodly passions.

How many leaders have been broken in board meetings standing alone? How many men and women of God have been fed messages of inadequacy, and are left feeling like total failures? These Tamars received their pain from the hands of those they served and loved.

Look at another thing that Tamar faced. After going through the pain of rape, Tamar faced an enemy that is far greater than the act itself. And that enemy is the enemy of rejection. This story of Tamar and Amnon gets right under my skin. It was not enough for her brother to rape and violate her against her innocent will, but he then turned right around and rejected her. After getting her alone, after she was raped, wounded, and violated, he then abandoned her as if he had no desire for her at all. Oh, my God — to be rejected and not wanted is one of the worst feelings that any human being could ever experience.

We know who is influencing these events. Because Amnon is not considering the heart or the mind of God, we know that it is nothing but the hand of Satan manipulating this situation. The old serpent the Devil — he is sick and I hate him with a passion! As if Tamar is not broken enough, he adds another nail to her coffin.

Amnon tells the servant to put her out. *2 Samuel 13:15-17 — Then Amnon hated her exceedingly; so that the hatred wherewith he hated her was greater than the love wherewith he had loved her. And Amnon said unto her, Arise, be gone. [16] And she said unto him, there is no cause: this evil in sending me away is greater than the other that thou didst unto me. But he would not hearken unto her. [17] Then he called his servant that ministered unto him, and said, Put now this woman out from me, and bolt the door after her.* Not only is Tamar broken, raped, and bruised, but now she is rejected. Wow! Tamar cries that the rejection is a greater evil than the initial act of the rape.

Rejection leaves you in a fetal position, helpless and depending on the individuals that you are connected to in order to supply you with the strength to continue to survive, yet these are the ones who abandon you the most. To be rejected and denied by the ones that you love, respect, and care for breaks every hope inside of you. There is nothing like being forsaken by the ones that you love and cherish. That is why rejection places you in a posture of helplessness and a sense of no development. It leaves you doubting everything that you are ever hoping to become. If you can't get the support of the people you respect and love, then who can you find comfort and security in?

Have you ever been on the outside looking in, hoping that the ones who have placed you out there would give you a chance? The most hurtful thing in my life was wanting to be accepted by the ones I respected, and it appeared that they found joy in keeping me out of their circle of influence. You hear things like, "You don't meet our standards"; "You're not the right type"; "You're not on our level"…and they cause you to feel as if you are not good enough, or that they had greater superior influence than me and I could never measure up to their standards.

But that is why Paul said in *2 Cor. 10:12 — For we dare not make ourselves of the number, or compare ourselves with some that commend themselves: but they measuring themselves by themselves, and comparing themselves among themselves, are not wise.* When we compare ourselves to each other, we will always see something that we lack in our own character. The truth of the matter is, we all have strengths and weaknesses. When we search for the strength in others and don't look at the strengths in ourselves, then we begin to feel inferior or inadequate because we neglect to see our strong points. Then, when we are rejected, it crushes us because no one wants to feel unwanted or unneeded. Instinctively, everyone wants to feel a sense of acceptance. Oh, my. What a day that must have been for Tamar...to feel unwanted in her pain. Doesn't it bring tears to your eyes?

I am sure that many are wondering how we survive. After hearing and feeling all of the pain and frustration, what do we do to not lose it all? The first thing that you must learn is that God will never lead you to a place where His grace cannot keep you. He will never allow you to wander in a place you cannot get out of. Remember, the fight is fixed and you always win. No matter what, with God you win.

So, you have to know that God is in total control. Know that the place you are in did not slip up on God. He knew the beginning from the end. He knew that you would be faced with the circumstances before you got there. He has already beforehand seen your pain.

Do not think that you are the only one ever faced with this situation. Remember that others have gone through the same pain and survived. This situation is not exclusive only to you. That is why in the book of *1 Cor. 10:13* it says ***There hath no temptation taken you but such as is common to man: but God is faithful, who will not suffer you to be tempted above that ye are able; but will with the temptation also make a way to escape, that ye may be able to bear it.***

Always remember that no matter how bad it gets, God has an escape route for you and you will come out all right. You can make it out of your pain. Just keep reading your story in life because it gets easier...if you will just remember to turn the page of your life's book and keep on reading. At the end of every good fairytale that you read, you discover that they lived happily ever after. Your latter shall be greater than your former if you don't throw in the towel and quit in the middle of your pain. Keep fighting and trusting God. At this point He is all you have to trust in.

Another thing that you must be confident in is when you have been violated, you haven't done anything to deserve the pain that you are experiencing. Don't take the blame for the one who caused the pain! It is not your fault. Don't allow them to make you become the *offender* when you are the one who was *offended*. Take charge of the situation and do not accept the guilt. Don't be afraid to confront the issue and accuse them of their offense by making statements like "you hurt me" or "you disappointed me" or "you violated me"...even if they are not there to hear the accusation, still charge them with what they did! But always remember when you have finished charging them, turn it loose and let it go!

By letting it go, it gives God an opportunity to give you something in return. The greatest thing about my relationship with God is I have discovered that nothing in my life has ever been wasted. With all of my painful experiences God has taken the pain and made me better. He has used my pain as a catalyst to recreate who and what I am to be and who I am to become. Believe it or not, my pain forced me to become a better person. I either said *I will never be like that and wound or hurt others*, or I said to myself *I will never accept a victim mentality again* and I fought for change. But whichever way the pain came, it shifted me to fight for a better me.

The next thing that you must decide is, *Do I want to hold on to it or do I want to let it go?* Because letting go is not an emotional thing, it is a choice. You may not feel like letting it go; you have to choose to let it go. And remember, it is a process. You have to make a continuous effort to tell yourself to let it go over and over again, and it may become a day-by-day choice. Or, it can become a minute-by-minute choice, but you have to keep choosing to release it until you are set free and the thing that is holding you no longer has any power over you. This is the part of the process that you have to decide to do.

Letting go of the one who hurt you is not easy. There will be days when you will want to hold on to the anger, bitterness, hatred, and frustration, because holding on to pain is easier than letting go.

Letting go means that you have to trust in someone greater than yourself, and that someone is God. It is like free-falling. When you decide to release the people that hurt you, then you have to trust that God will make everything better for you. It requires that you see a bigger and better future.

Trusting God redirects your view of life. It causes you to focus on the positive and delete the negative. In other words, when you let go of the person who hurt you, you can see a better you. Seeing a better you will permit you to see God in a greater capacity. And He will give you a healthier life. Your life will become full and productive and bear much fruit. God will release greater for you. So, you can make a choice to hold on to the pain and allow it to control you and eventually destroy you, or release the pain and allow God to heal you from the offense, which will unchain you from the offender.

The next thing you must learn is to give God glory in all things. There is a song that comes to my mind at this time. This song is by Kurt Carr which says: *I almost let go, I felt like I just couldn't take life anymore. My problems had me bound. Depression weighed me down. But God held me close, so I wouldn't let go. God's mercy kept me, so I wouldn't let go. I almost gave up. I was right at the edge of a breakthrough, but couldn't see it The Devil really had me; but Jesus came and grabbed me, and He held me close, So I wouldn't let go. God's mercy kept me, so I wouldn't let go. So I'm here today because God kept me. I'm alive today, only because of His grace. Oh, he kept me so I*

wouldn't let go.

Remember, it is at the darkest moments in your life that God refuses to let go. He holds you close and He deserves the glory and the praise for just coming through for you.

Any time you are pushed beyond your mental, emotional, and physical capacity, which causes your wounds to go deep, and you survive, you have a reason to give God glory because you should realize that it is God who has brought you through. Coming through the storms of life gives you a greater glimpse of His glory. And seeing His power and His glory should give you a reason to give Him praise. So, then you have been given an opportunity to become an instrument of praise. It is through your experiences that you have a testimony of how He brought you out, and will give Him glory and honor. It is from you coming forth out of your experiences that you are able to give God praise and share with others your victory.

Let's pray:

Father, in the name of Jesus, Lord we thank You for taking us through some of the most difficult times of our lives. If it had not been for You we don't know what would have become of our destiny and our future. It was You who covered us in our pain. It was Your love that sustained us through all of the disappointment and frustration. We were completely

lost in hatred, anger, and bitterness. It was as if we were lost in the valley and could not find our way out. And even while in the valley we were surrounded by wild beasts that kept us frightened and dismayed. But You, being the Good Shepherd that You are, came and rescued us and brought us out of our fears and pain. Lord, life without You is not worth living — not even for one day, God. You are our only hope and source. The pain of unforgiveness is more than we can conceive or bear. We need You to deliver us and set our hearts and minds free. You are the one we look to. You are the one we depend on. And You are the only one who can deliver us. So Lord, begin now to work on our hearts and give us the strength to let go of the people who have hurt us. We no longer want to carry them as a weight that is weighing our life down and hindering us from being the best that we can be. God, this is greater than we are and now, Lord, we surrender it to You because if we give it to You, we know and believe that You can and will fix it for us. We love You, Lord, and we don't want anything stopping our relationship with You. So, God, heal our families. Heal our churches. Heal our communities. Heal our nation. And most of all, Lord, heal our world. We love You, Lord, and we look to You. These things we pray in the name of Jesus.

Amen

Chapter Thirteen
Drop the Charges and Forgive You!

Tamar Identified Her Own Pain — 2 Samuel 13:18-22

[18] And she had a garment of divers colours upon her: for with such robes were the king's daughters that were virgins apparelled. Then his servant brought her out, and bolted the door after her.

[19] And Tamar put ashes on her head, and rent her garment of divers colours that was on her, and laid her hand on her head, and went on crying. [20] And Absalom her brother said unto her, Hath Amnon thy brother been with thee? but hold now thy peace, my sister: he is thy brother; regard not this thing. So Tamar remained desolate in her brother Absalom's house.

[21] But when king David heard of all these things, he was very wroth. [22] And Absalom spake unto his brother Amnon neither good nor bad: for Absalom hated Amnon, because he had forced his sister Tamar.

Tamar wore a robe that spoke and identified who she was. She wore a robe of many colors, signifying her status and position in the kingdom morally and relational. Due to circumstances beyond her control, and the mere fact that she was violated by her own brother, the anguish of these events caused her to rip her own identity. It was by her own hands that she revealed her plight and her pain. Pain will cause you to turn on yourself and take away the very framework of your identity. It will cause you to lose yourself in the process.

The agony of being raped and rejected caused Tamar to rend her royal garments, as a depiction of a sense of grief. Her heartache became unbearable — so much so that she put ashes on her head, which symbolized mourning, and she felt unworthy to wear her royal attire. When sorrow enters, it can cause you to become so submerged in your unhappiness that you forget there is more life to be lived.

Pain will allow you to lose yourself, who you were born to be, and who you were born to become. Yes, the violation of Tamar left her broken and caused her great pain. But it was sadness that re-identified Tamar that day. That is the reason I am declaring that Tamar announced the pain of her ill-treatment. It was Tamar's heartache that moved her to strip herself of her identity and lose sight of the plan that God had for her life.

I would never want, for one minute, to play down Tamar's anguish. What she experienced was horrendous, and no one should ever have to go through that type of abuse and suffering at the hands of a loved one. I am sure that day Tamar not only lost her virginity, but her life's vitality changed drastically. Life threw her a curve ball that was very difficult for her to catch.

When life sucker-punches you, I am sure you are wondering what to do. How do you bounce back? You ask yourself, *Where do I go from here? How do I pick up the pieces after the pain? Who do I turn to? How do I survive the storm?* The only real and absolute answer that I have is for you to place yourself in the hands of God. He is the only one who will ever be able to make sense of the chaos. No matter how dreadful the situations became that I have faced in my life, it was the love, grace, and the mercy of God that were able to make sense out of the things in my life that made absolutely no sense. He was the one who picked up all of the fragmented pieces. He knew where everything belonged and placed my life back in order, and I say thank You, Jesus.

If you think you can do it without Him, I am here to tell you it will never work. You are not strong enough, nor are you wise enough or smart enough. Your money or your fame cannot handle the emptiness that is in your broken heart. The only one who can do it is God, because no matter how hard you try, you will never see everything the way God sees it. God sees past our pain, disappointment, and our grief, and He knows how to get to the core of the matter. He knows what it takes to heal a wounded spirit because that is what He specializes in. When our souls are overwhelmed with grief, that is when we need God to restore and heal us. We just do not have the power nor the ability. That is why we so desperately need God.

Without God's intervention, sisters and brothers, grief will re-identify you. It takes God to carry you through the pain and sorrow. He gives you clear instruction on how to survive. Trust me, you never want to go through the rough seasons of your life without Him. And being without Him during these painful instances will cause you to take on characteristics that you would have never normally accepted. Remember that it is God who gives you the strength to fight the things that are fighting you.

God is well-equipped in handling every broken place in your heart, mind, body, and your soul. He is a master in reconstructive surgery, and that is the very thing that a broken and wounded heart needs. It needs a complete and total makeover, and the only one who can handle the job is Jesus Christ. When you have been greatly wounded by someone, and you leave the wounds unattended, these injuries lead to far greater complications in other areas of your life.

Grief leaves you with depression. It leaves you with feelings of rejection. It causes you to develop inferiority complexes and many more destructive behaviors. It will cause you to devalue who you are and it will cause you to devalue others. It will leave you with feelings of defeat, and these feelings will begin to dominate your life. It will cause you to behave in ways that you would never dream you would behave, and do things that you would never in a million years dream of doing.

A baby is not born believing and aspiring to become a drug addict, a bum, a murderer, a child abuser, a rapist, a prostitute, or a failure. It was somewhere during the difficult sharp turns of the baby's life, a turn that they were not prepared to handle, that the child's perspective changed and they began to take on the nature of their environment. And because of these painful and hurtful events, it changed that individual, and those changes caused them to develop their unhealthy characteristics.

As I said once before, I believe that the people, places, and things that we associate with influence who we will become. It can influence you negatively or positively. But regardless, when we look close enough we discover more times than not that we are a product of our environment. We live our lives according to what we hear and see. And I would daresay that whatever good or bad experiences we find ourselves in, these experiences shape who we are. Most often our unhealthy qualities were learned through our painful experiences.

That is why I want you to see clearly the destruction that grief causes. It clouds your decisions and your ability to make sound judgments. It causes you to become stagnant and leaves you without the ability to reach your full potential. It chokes the life out of you. It changes the way that you see life and the way that life sees you. That is why the grief that Tamar felt left her wounded, embarrassed, humiliated, and broken. The evil that was done to her caused her to be ashamed. Tamar bore the shame of her plight when she was the one who was viciously betrayed and raped.

A lot of people today are wearing the aroma and the stench of their cruel abusers and the ones who hurt them the most. They have taken the behavior of the people that caused them the greatest pain and are now acting, looking, and thinking just like those who neglected and violated them. They are still carrying the odor of the offender, and because they will not let the person or the act go, the one that was offended has metamorphosed into the personality of the one who offended them, and now they look alike.

When you don't turn things loose when you should, you begin to take on the nature of the thing that you are holding on to. You begin to become cruel, cynical, distrusting, pessimistic, suspicious, sarcastic, and very skeptical. That is why you must Drop the Charges and Forgive Yourself so that you can be free — free to live and free to love.

I am sure that before the events that left Tamar in this dreadful situation, she viewed her life from a far more exciting and adventurous perspective. How could she not see herself living a life full of fun and excitement? After all, she was the king's kid. Tamar was born into a royal lineage and everything about her displayed royalty. All of her life she was groomed for royalty. They taught her how to enter and exit a room. She knew the etiquette of her royal position in the kingdom. Nothing that was of significant value or class was withheld from her. She was given everything she needed to become who she was predestined to be. She was taught grace and class to the highest degree. Remember, this was David's daughter. Her father was a great warrior and one of the greatest kings ever known. When she entered a room, her very presence demanded attention. The mere essence of her countenance suggested that she was exceptional in beauty. After all, it was her beauty and her virginity that caused her brother Amnon to desire her.

Her royal attire signified her pedigree and it identified who her father was. The colors of her garments said to every eligible suitor that she was morally kept. This garment that Tamar wore gave her privileges that ordinary individuals would never be able to obtain. It let everyone know that she was an heir to a king. Before this painful experience, the grace of her inherited garment exemplified that she walked in places that only the royal seed could.

Doesn't that describe the children of God? When we give our lives to Christ and submit to the plan of God and accept Jesus Christ as Lord and Savior, then the blood of Jesus becomes every believer's garment to identify us as heirs and joint heirs of Christ. We become a part of a royal priesthood — a holy nation and a peculiar people. We become the sons and daughters of the King of Kings and the Lord of Lords. We are His children. When we accept Jesus Christ as Lord and Savior, then His blood is the royal garment that covers our sinful flesh and sinful nature. His *blood* allows us the full privilege to stand in the royal courts of our Heavenly Father. It lets us come boldly before the throne of grace and fall down at the mercy seat. It gives us full authority to stand in the presence of our Father, who is our King, ruler, and Lord.

And as we stand in the presence of our King, the oil of His glory which He anoints us with identifies who we are. When we stand among the ungodly, our royal attire speaks loud and clear for itself. It screams that these are the children of God!

And God covers us with His glory, which is His goodness. It is our signet and our seal that says we have been in the presence of our King and we are heavenly citizens. I want you to know that the only way you can stand in His presence is by being covered under His *blood*. That is why it is impossible to stand in the presence of a King and not be clothed in royal attire, which is the *blood of Jesus*.

Another thing that you must understand is when you stand in the presence of our Father, be prepared to be changed. You cannot stand in the presence of a King and have your life remain the same. Just the awe of who He is will redirect everything in your life. That is why you must expect to be changed. The glory of God will always create a transformation within us. His glory demands immediate change because it is His glory that alters the hearts and the minds of people and gives us the desire to be like Him.

God also covers us with His righteousness, and the world and demons see our righteous garments. Out of all the gifts of God, I love this one the most. God, through His son, Jesus Christ, paid the price for our sins, and counted us as righteous. In other words, He placed us back into a right relationship with Him.

And righteousness is another gift of mercy that He gives to us to identify that we are His children. No, we can never pay for it or work for it. It is a gift freely given to us by God. The only thing we must do is accept it. By accepting the gift of God, we become His sons and daughters. Then and only then do we have access and privileges to everything in God's Kingdom. It says that we are covered and protected by our Father, the King that rules Heaven and earth. And along with everything that God offers, He has assigned the angelic host to assist us, also.

That is why when I look at Tamar, and knowing that she was a king's kid, I understand that the girl had everything she needed. Not only everything that she needed, but she was given access to everything in the kingdom. Tamar was well-equipped to become any and everything that she could possibly desire to be. But there was one thing that broke her and stood in her way, and it was the awful act of a senseless loved one, her selfish brother, Amnon. This one incident blindsided poor Tamar to the point that she was unable to regroup. Oftentimes our painful experiences catch us off-guard.

Tamar was well-equipped in every area of life except the one area that changed her life forever. And that is, how do you handle unexpected pain from a loved one? I am sure she was very astute in her culture because she was royalty. But the one thing she lacked was the one tool that she needed the most. And that was how to survive a horrible attack from someone that you trust and love. Oh, my. She was just not prepared for the pain. And when we really think about it, no one is ever prepared for pain and rejection.

When you really love and care for someone and they hurt you, it leaves you numb and lifeless. It stabs you right in the heart. It clouds your thinking and your ability to give sound reasoning. It leaves you stuck in a place that continues to remind you of the insensitive act of rejection betrayal and agony. It leaves you wondering, *What did I do to deserve such a cruel display of distrust?* It consumes everything that is within you and it sucks the life right out of you. The bright gleam in your eyes becomes a dull flicker. And this kind of pain is just something that only time can heal.

That is why many times when we are offended we are never prepared for the offense; many times we love and respect the people who offend us, and no matter how much we do to prepare for it, it always seems to catch us off-guard. If you are like me, I never want to believe that the people I love will hurt me. That is why it hurts so badly because we often experience the offense from the hands of the ones we love and respect the most.

Tamar's pain drove her to rip her royal attire. At that moment she could not see who she was because the only thing that she could feel was her pain. I am begging you — no matter what comes your way, please do not lose yourself in the pain or the process. Hold on to hope, and hold on to the promises of God regardless of what happens in your life.

The bible tells us that God will be with us even until the end of the world. When we become God's sons and daughters, we automatically receive the strength to fight the good fight of faith. And faith is what will cause you to win because He has given to us victory. Read it. It is at the end of the book. Just check out the last chapter of the Word of God. It's in there. Read the bible and you will see. No matter what we go through or what we face, we win in the end. It is our inheritance in the Kingdom of God. Nothing can strip that away from us. The only way we lose our inheritance is we walk away from it and never pick it up again. And walking away from God is not an easy thing to do. What you must remember is it is not you who is totally in love with Him; it is Him that is totally and completely in love with you. God is obsessed with humanity and His love is stronger than we can even imagine.

So you see, it is hard work to go to Hell and be without Him. Jesus said He wished that none would perish, but that all would come to repentance. It has never been God's desire to be separated from us. It was we who became separated from Him. That is why when you look at the real picture, it takes a lot of effort to not love and obey God. You have to reject all the love that He gives. Ignore the grace that He applies. Walk away from the mercy that He shows; forsake the goodness that He displays; refuse the peace that He offers; disallow the compassion that He presents; and even at that God will continue to compel us to return back to Him so that we can receive the promise. As I said before, you have to really work hard to go to Hell.

That is why throughout these writings I have continued to remind you that we, as believers of Jesus Christ, are the blood-bought children of God. We are robed in His righteousness. The scarlet blood of Jesus is the color that allows everyone to identify us with our inheritance as the children of a King. And as His children, it is up to us to maintain our garments. Our pain can take us away, or our pain can pull us closer to Him.

In this story of Tamar, it lets us know that although we are in the Kingdom of God, we still face moments of hateful and bitter calculated plots and painful wounds by the hands of those we love and trust. It is up to us to decide what we will do with the painful pitfalls that we face every day of our lives. It is not fair, but guess what? It is the hand that we are dealt.

Tamar's life was interrupted by pain, embarrassment, and rejection. The trap was set and Tamar was ensnared by the underlying plan that the enemy used to plot and destroy her future. So you see, Satan has been in the background all along. It is his heart's desire to see our lives full of hate and bitterness because that is the way that he is. He wants us to be like him and not be like God, who is full of love and compassion. Satan hates God and he wants us to do the same. That is why he hates anything or anyone that loves God.

When you look closely at this story, there was a greater source behind the scenes than the unhealthy love and lust of a brother. There was a major plot. And Amnon was just the tool or the vehicle that was used to stop Tamar from reaching her destiny and receiving the real plans that God had for her life.

What you must know is nothing just happens. It saddens me to read that, at that point, Tamar became a victim and a prisoner of her circumstances. She yielded all of her dreams and aspirations and surrendered them to her prison of pain. She found herself, at that moment, too weak to pull past her circumstances and her tragedy.

Her brother Absalom said to her, "Regard not this thing." In other words, what Absalom was saying was act like it didn't happen and be silent about it, because he is your brother. Let's not embarrass the family's name. Keep it quiet. Look at what else she had to endure. Now she had to save the reputation of the family at the expense of her pain. She was told to keep her mouth shut. This was a time of great pain and sorrow...and they were asking her to preserve the reputation of their family? I am sure Tamar was saying to herself, *Can I please get a break? Will someone please cut me some slack?*

I want to ask you, how many secrets have you kept in order not to embarrass the one who hurt you, just so your family would not be destroyed? As if what you have gone through was not enough! I know you are saying, "Now I have to bear my pain in silence." How many secrets are you carrying that are killing you from within?

Yes, there are times when victims are asked not to tell. I want you to remember, even if you choose to keep the incident a secret and take an oath of silence. I want to leave you with hope. You must clearly see that there is someone you can talk to, and His name is Jesus. You can drop your secret off at the feet of Jesus, and forgive yourself. He knows what to do with those dirty little secrets and He won't tell a soul. No, He won't tell anyone about it. God says that you can trust Him. He promises to keep your secret so you no longer have to. Drop the charges and forgive yourself.

When you are in the middle of a battle, it is not the time to take an oath of silence. It is your opportunity to cry out to God and plead for His help! He will reveal to you how to let it go! You must learn to forgive yourself, even if you are not at fault. Drop the Charges and Forgive Yourself!

Holding on to pain longer than it needs to stay will cause decay in your life.

It is when you refuse to let it go that it begins to eat you from the inside out. Yes, you are hurt and very discouraged, but put your hope and trust in God and He will give you the courage to overcome your pain. You must willingly and consciously, every day of your life, let it go.

Unforgiveness is like cancer. It will aggressively and painfully kill you and everyone and everything around you. That is why it is important to forgive yourself, because until you can really forgive yourself and go free, you can never understand what it is like to forgive others.

That is why I believe in the prayer that Jesus taught. When He said "forgive us our trespasses as we forgive others their trespasses" He knew that we must first feel what it means to need forgiveness ourselves before we can honestly and sincerely learn to forgive others. We must understand the burden and agony of being the offender before we can apply true forgiveness. When we forgive ourselves, we release the burden and guilt that it carries. Then and only then will we really understand what real freedom is. Once we learn to freely accept God's forgiveness, we will learn to freely give others our forgiveness. It is all in the order of God.

Isn't it amazing that Tamar's brother tells her not to lose heart over it when everything that she was and ever hoped to be was destroyed in one day by one act of humiliation and violation? Her brother Absalom, I am sure because of his love for his sister, was trying at that moment to bring her comfort by letting her know that he would be with her through this pain. We can get through this together. I am sure he was saying, "I am here for you." And that is what our Father wants me to tell you — no matter what you go through, He is here for you and we can get through your place of pain together.

It saddens me that the story ends like this, because this is the part of the story where Tamar resorts to living the remainder of her days in her brother's house, desolate. And because of her pain, she became isolated, deserted, barren, and unfruitful. I want to cry at this point because Tamar lost who she was because of her circumstance. She was unable to pull herself out of the pain that she experienced. She lost her fight.

Whatever you do, please don't lose your fight. You must continue to fight to overcome your condition and circumstances. The choice that Tamar made at that point was to no longer choose to produce. She shut down her womb to give birth. She allowed nothing to come in and nothing to get out. It was then that she emptied her dreams, passions, and desires. She lost the sparkle in her eyes to love, dream, and pursue every dream and purpose that God had planned for her life. This one act placed her in a personal prison in which she closed the door on herself and life.

Could her outcome have been different if, at some point in her pain, she decided to forgive herself and her violator, thereby allowing the healing process of God to mend and restore what was torn apart and what was broken? Remember, Tamar tore her own royal garments.

Let's pray:

Father, in the name of Jesus, I am so grateful that You love and care about us the way that You do. Help us now to see the importance of forgiving others as You have forgiven us. Our lives come with many disappointments, pain, and rejection. Some of the scars are so deep that only You can heal them. We look to You, oh God, to guard our hearts so that we won't lose our passion for life and living. Train us and teach us to love one another as You have loved us. Place in our hearts to love those who spitefully mistreat us. Let us learn to forgive even when forgiving hurts. Let us see the benefits of letting things go so that they cannot destroy our dreams, visions, and passion for pursuing life and love. Teach us to run to You in our times of trouble and help us to understand that You are the one who can make sense of it all. Take pride out of our hearts and give us the spirit of humility and kindness. Continue to kindle the fight within us and let us believe in who we are, and show us how to trust in who we are. Let us clearly see that the whole Kingdom of God is going in front of us to defeat our enemies. And that You are our reward.

Because Isaiah 52:12 says **But you will not go out in haste, Nor will you go as fugitives; For the Lord will go before you, And the God of Israel will be your rear guard.** *Thank You, Lord, for being our Father, Ruler, and our King. We love You,*

Lord. Please, Lord, heal the nations with the writing of this manuscript and let everyone who reads it find themselves in the pages of this book, and begin the healing process within us. Oh Lord, our strength and our redeemer! These things I ask in the name of Jesus Christ our Lord.

Amen

Drop the Charges and Forgive You!

About the Author

Joyce Hawkins is the Founder and CEO of Mending Broken Bridges Ministries in Toledo, Ohio. She is an author and teacher, beloved mother and mentor, and a spirit-led preacher of God's Word. Joyce was raised in Pontiac, Michigan, by her loving parents Lenon and Bettie Clark, who worked very hard to provide a stable environment for their five children. Joyce was the youngest of the family. At the age of 30 she surrendered her life to God. Shortly thereafter, God revealed to her His desire for her to preach and teach His Word around the world.

In 2005, God gave Joyce the name of Mending Broken Bridges Ministries and the vision for it. It was through her suffering that God reminded her that no matter what you go through in life, there is still hope, and the cross of Calvary firmly remains the bridge that will safely bring all of humanity into their destiny. Joyce believes that just as God has shown us the love that He has for us, it is now our responsibility to display that same love to each other. We become the bridges that God uses to mend the brokenhearted. She officially launched Mending Broken Bridges Ministries in 2011 with a conference in the City of Toledo, Ohio.

By sharing her many stories of overcoming tragedy and finding victory and restoration through the power of Christ, she has impacted people from every walk of life around the world. Whether men, women, or children; business executives, currently unemployed, or college students; wealthy, or impoverished; hopeful or in despair, Joyce Hawkins can relate to them all, and through her transparent and heartfelt love of God, they can relate to her.